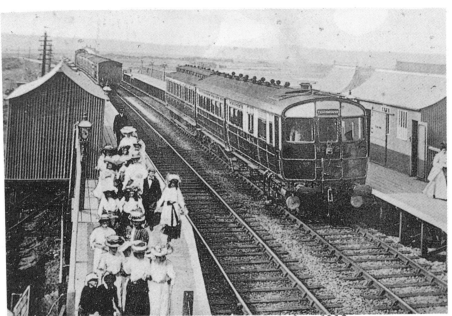
Steam rail-motor leaving Dawlish Warren, before 1910

Cover: Leaving Torquay Station for Paignton, May 1892

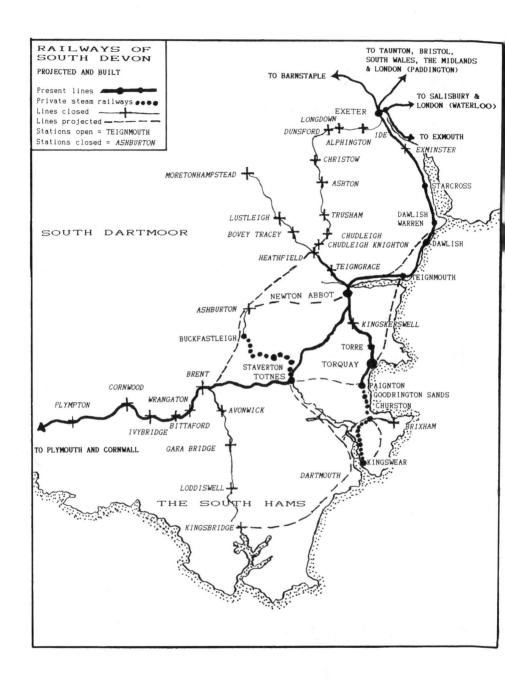

IRON HORSE TO THE SEA

Railways in South Devon

John Pike

EX LIBRIS PRESS

First published in 1987 by
Ex Libris Press
1 The Shambles
Bradford on Avon
Wiltshire

Cover by 46 Design, Bradford on Avon
Typeset in 11 on 13 point Plantin
by Saxon Printing Ltd., Derby
Printed by A. Wheaton and Co. Ltd., Exeter

ISBN 0 948578 12 2

For my grandson Stephen, already a railway enthusiast

Note: Acts of Parliament are identified by the regnal year of the Sovereign; together with a Chapter number (abbreviated 'c'), hence 38 Vict.c.38 = Torbay & Brixham Railway Act, 1875. These are included, where appropriate, in the text.

Note on the illustrations
These illustrations have been collected over a period of nearly 20 years. Many were found in the extensive *Pictorial Records* at Torquay Museum. Others are from the former Torbay Borough Archives (now in the care of Devon Library Services at Torquay). The remainder were lent to me for copying; these are acknowledged individually. My thanks to them all.

J.P.

CONTENTS

Foreword

If ever an area of Britain has been changed by the coming of the railway it is the South Devon coast from the Exe to the Dart. East of the Exe the old Great Western ran miles from the sea and although the later-arriving London and South-Western is closer it only reached down to the coast with small branch lines. West of the Dart the railway gets nowhere near the sea until Plymouth, so that the coast there is comparatively untouched by the tourist trade.

The turnpike roads to Exmouth and Torquay first created the resorts of South Devon, but it was the coming of the railway - the main line actually following the coast from Dawlish to Teignmouth; the Torbay branch from Torquay to Paignton - that really saw these places grow. In the early days it was the aristocracy and the upper middle class who could afford holidays when these resorts were frequented mainly during the winter. Since the First World War, with the growth of holidays with pay, these resorts have become accessible to all and are now among the most popular in Britain. Indeed, of the millions who flock to Devon every summer, a half of them are concentrated along a stretch of coast from the mouth of the Exe to the mouth of the Dart.

The peak in Torbay's popularity was in 1958, before the motor car ousted the railway as the main means of transport. For a few weeks in August every year some 30,000 people would arrive by train each Saturday. Ten trains an hour, each of 12 to 15 coaches, streamed through Whiteball Tunnel, the railway gate to the West. In the morning peaks this number would increase to a train every three minutes; trains queued to disgorge their passengers at Paignton.

It all began with the railways - trains still carry a great many people to holiday in the area - and holidays have led to large numbers of retirement homes. The social explosion caused by the coming of the railways is the story John Pike unfolds in these pages. He is a careful and painstaking historian, and his survey of the railways of South Devon deserves the widest readership.

Crispin Gill, OBE
August 1987

7

The 'Romantic Railway' through the eyes of the artist, Dawlish c.1846

Between Teignmouth and Newton Abbot, 1850/5
The old wooden Shaldon-Teignmouth toll bridge is shown

Introduction

The railway arrived in South Devon nearly a century and a half ago; it caused a minor population explosion, changed the local people's way of life and helped set a pattern of urban development which was completely different from the 'old country life' which had existed for generations. The coastline between the Exe and the Teign has been disfigured by a line running along the edge of the sands and through the gaunt red sandstone cliffs ever since - to the detriment of the scenery - but what a wonderful sight the sea must have been to the early visitors who flocked to the watering places which grew up so rapidly. Indeed that sight still thrills visitors in the late twentieth century.

In support of a proposed railway extension in the 1850s a petition stated, of Torquay residents, that 'an unusually large number consist of gentry, many of whom are invalids resorting to Torquay for the sake of the climate'. Like its neighbours much of its prosperity derived from those who came to bathe, or just to enjoy the scenery, but as the Victorian period was coming to its end it was politic to encourage the healthy as well as the ailing to come west. The 'holiday resort' was born and millions of holidaymakers came by rail over the next 80 years. Devonians were enabled to move out as well: the railway made it easier and cheaper; some went to the more prosperous parts of Britain, others to the seaports for passages to the Empire and the USA.

Whilst the seaside towns flourished, inland communities declined rapidly and dramatically. As W.G.Hoskins points out in his history of Devon, the coming of the railway killed a number of ancient market towns, which had existed since the twelfth century, as it had removed their *raison d'etre*, particularly where the lines passed them by. As will be shown later the coach and wagon traffic disappeared too - sometimes almost overnight - and led to the demise of the trades associated with it.

However, just as the coming of the railway ousted horse-drawn conveyances so the motor car, and foreign holidays, have meant the decline of the railway - in South Devon Doctor Beeching's axe which severed the Paignton to Kingswear section and the Totnes to Ashburton branch has given private enterprise the chance of resurg-

9

ence. The Dart Valley Railway and the Torbay and Dartmouth Railway bring past glories into the present and give thousands the chance of a real journey by train. - the sound of steam engines beating their way up the slopes from the River Dart towards Churston brings pleasure to 'children' of all ages.

Things however might have been very different. Entrepreneurs have tried at various times to extend the railway over the Dart in the vicinity of Dittisham - this would have taken the main line through to Plymouth and Cornwall. The South Hams, that quiet and rural landscape between Totnes and the sea, would have been in the hands of developers for well over a century. Those who like their Devon scenery unspoilt should pass a vote of thanks to those who had the foresight to stop them.

This is principally the story of the Great Western in South Devon; men were proud to 'work on the Railway', in some families for three or four generations. Passengers too thought highly of the GWR and treated its staff as personal friends.

Station staff at Torre Station posing for photographer, 1865

I   GOING PLACES

First 'Rail-Road' Plans.

The Turnpike era had brought a minor revolution to Devon; in the second half of the eighteenth century local people had seen their traditional conveyances of goods, the packhorses, replaced by horse-drawn carts. In many places the sight of a wheeled vehicle had only just ceased to be a novelty. In the next 50 years coaches, including the Royal Mail, were running into the County and on from Exeter to Plymouth - taking about 14 hours for the journey. In South Devon, the Napoleonic Wars had brought the first 'incomers' - families of naval officers joining their husbands ashore from the Fleet blockading Brest, and the first visitors, many with delicate lungs, coming to bathe in the warm sea-water. Whilst some of the gentry had their private carriages, most had to come to the watering-places by stage-coach over rough highways. In the early 1830s the journey from Exeter to Torquay through Chudleigh took four hours; around the coast via Teignmouth it took rather longer.

Interest in railways began early in the West Country. In 1824 there were several serious proposals to link Bristol with London and its neighbour Bath. Three companies were formed: the Bath & Bristol Railway, the London and Bristol Railroad and the Grand Western Railway, but all failed. The reality of a railway came with the opening of the Stockton and Darlington in 1825. Much nearer home Dymond noted the same year:

This was the period when the question of Rail Roads was first mooted in this part of the country. Public meetings were called and propositions adopted for the formation of them to and from Exeter. One was proposed to be made from Taunton to Exeter; another from Exeter to Exmouth; with a capital of £40,000 in £50 shares.[1]

This was seven years before the group of Bristol merchants met to consider building a railway from London to their City. That gathering took place in the autumn of 1832 but that too was after the first decisions had been taken in South Devon. A meeting held in Newton Abbot on 14 August was told by the promoters that the 'projected railroad between Torquay, Newton and Ashburton is now likely to be speedily proceeded with'. There is no record of the proceedings but the plans for one between Newton and Torquay only, first announced on the 6 December in the *Exeter Flying Post*, were deposited with the Clerk of the Peace. [2] Its readers were told that 'it is in contemplation to form a railroad between Newton and Torquay for the purpose of facilitating inter-course between the former town and that port.' The plan, immaculately drawn by James Green, the civil engineer best known for his work on bridges and canals (he was Devon county bridge surveyor from 1808 to 1834[3]), shows that the line was to commence in Newton Abbot, pass by way of Longaford Bridge to the Mill at Kingskerswell then follow, more or less, the new Turnpike road to Tor where it would pass through the middle of the village then, following the line of the river Fleet past the old Mill, terminate at a point near Cary Green. As with so many schemes in early Torquay, the document was signed by William Kitson as well. The scheme came to nought and it was over ten years before further moves were made.

There was a third very early attempt to bring the railway into South Devon; the existence of the **Totnes, Ashburton and Buckfastleigh Rail-Road** has just come to light during a search of the Duke of Somerset's papers.[4] 'Surveyed and lithoged by C. Dean [on] 14th October 1833' it is headed First Report and commences: 'I was led to enquire how far the proposed Rail-Road to Torquay was practicable, and being satisfied of its utter impracticability for locomotive Engines, and that it could not be effected without an enormous outlay of capital, I was induced to make the present survey from Ashburton to Totnes'.

The line would commence at Ballard Lime-Kilns (north of Ashburton) and end on the east bank of the Dart below Bridgetown. One problem of the time would be prevented, the report promised as 'Cyder will be conveyed on shipboard with no risque of second fermentation.' Other traffic confidently expected would be culm, coal and iron. It was many years before further moves were made for a railway between Ashburton and Totnes and when it was built it followed closely Dean's route.

The story of the building of the Great Western Railway from London to Bristol has been told many times.[5] 'God's Wonderful Railway' was built by Isambard Kingdom Brunel on broad gauge tracks; the Bristol to Bath and the London to Maidenhead sections opening in 1838 and the complete London-Bristol in 1841. Even when the great man was heavily engaged on this he found time to survey the proposed route of a line which was to link Exeter with Plymouth. The first indication that there was a determination to bring the railway into Devon appears in the *Exeter & Plymouth Gazette* in November 1835 when a meeting of the **Exeter, Plymouth and Devonport Railway Company** was reported. This initiative has had a profound effect on South Devon ever since. If Plymouth had not existed the railway would never have come in the way and at the time it did - and with its passenger traffic being the largest revenue earner since, the line has remained viable right up to the present time. When however a railway to Exeter became a reality following the passing of the Bristol & Exeter Railway Act, the plans which were deposited were for the **London, Exeter and Falmouth Railway**; the idea for building a railway in isolation had gone for good.

Later in 1836 Brunel was in South Devon[6] mapping the route, possibly for this Company, for a line from the Bristol & Exeter's proposed terminus at St Davids which crossed the Teign near Shaldon and passed close to Torquay: after bridging the Dart it would sweep through the South Hams to complete a direct line to Plymouth. It was probably during this time that he first saw and fell in love with Watcombe near Torquay. Eleven years later he bought the land from local squire Hercules Brown; it was on a southward facing slope with panoramic views overlooking Torbay and it was here he resolved to build his 'dream house' and live out his last days as a country squire

13

too. Probably because of finance not being forthcoming nothing came of this scheme either and it was some years before railway mania gripped Devon.

On 1 May 1844 trains arrived in Devon when the **Bristol and Exeter Railway** was completed as far as Exeter. This story is told in detail elsewhere.[7] However, a year before this, in 1843, the prospectus was issued for the **Plymouth, Devonport and Exeter Railway**. Very much aimed at improving the economy of Plymouth it stated the proposed line would be 51½ miles long, and that 'its course combines with the largest amount of local accommodation, less engineering difficulties than are found to exist on either of the other lines which have been projected'. It further indicated to investors that much of the finance was being provided by the Great Western, the Bristol and Gloucester and the Bristol and Exeter. The events which led up to the formation of this Company started in 1840 when a survey was made of three possible routes from Plymouth to Exeter.[8] One, 37 miles long, described as the 'direct route', was an extraordinary proposal which involved the use of ropes and water-wheels to haul the carriages on to the high moor passing Warren House Inn on the southern part of Dartmoor. This involved the building of two huge reservoirs near Princetown and others in the vicinity of the East Dart. Interest not surprisingly waned and the southern route became the preferred one. Which one of the two proposed, inland or coast, became the next question which had to be answered. The story is told[9] that what was perhaps the first 'traffic survey', was conducted in both Newton and Ashburton

to ascertain which route bore the most traffic, and for that purpose men were stationed near St Leonard's Tower for three weeks, in order to keep a record of the number of people passing there during that period, while other men were stationed at a certain point in Ashburton for a similar time and purpose. At Ashburton those interested actually ran cabs out of the town and back again, and anyone could have a free drive; the idea being to increase the traffic, and make it appear as heavy as possible in order to get the railway cut through Ashburton. But it was found that the people passing through Newton far exceeded those going through Ashburton, and this consideration, backed by the fact that if the Ashburton route was taken, Teignmouth and Torquay, as well as Newton would be cut off, decided the directors to cut the line along its present route.

Meetings at Plymouth and Newton at the end of 1843 confirmed the abandonment of the Dartmoor scheme. One of the changes also agreed was to bring the line in a large semi-circle to the west of Forde House instead of east of it as originally intended. The Bill went before Parliament and in the following March as part of the procedure 'Mr Walker arrived in Exeter; having been appointed by the Lords of Admiralty to report on the line of the South Devon Railway (the name had been changed to this before then) along the estuaries of the Exe and the Teign'. Their Lordships obviously exercised authority over matters not strictly of their concern; nevertheless modifications were adopted at his suggestion, the line being routed nearer the coast than Brunel originally intended. On 1 July 1844 the South Devon Railway Act (7 & 8 Vict. c.68) received Royal Assent. This line from Exeter to Plymouth was to run from Teignmouth along the north bank of the River Teign to Newton then south-west to Totnes so that the nearest this would approach the Torbay towns was at Aller just south of Newton Abbot. The Chief engineer was to be Mr Brunel and the track 'broad gauge'. The full story of the result of this decision will be told in the next chapter.

'Railway Mania' in South Devon
Almost immediately attention turned to the need to put Dartmouth and Torbay on the railway map. In October a survey for a railway from Newton to Torquay harbour was started. In the same month a meeting was held at the Globe Hotel at Newton which was 'largely attended by gentlemen interested in the land and trade of the neighbourhood' and a committee was appointed. In November Parliamentary notice was advertised which described the line 'as commencing at Aller and terminating at Torquay harbour through Torre and by way of Union and Fleet Streets'. The prospectus announced it as the **Torquay & Newton Railway Company**. Messrs Kitsons were the solicitors and

Robert Dymond was appointed engineer. Although plans were deposited[10] it never progressed beyond this stage. The plan shows that it was intended to follow approximately the route proposed in 1832 but at St Michaels instead of following the course described in the Notice it turned to the south-east along the line of the Turnpike road to Paignton [Avenue Road] to the sands near Torre Abbey from whence a Tramway to the Pier Head was to be constructed. The *Notes prepared in support of Plans for a Torquay to Newton Railway*, also deposited, offered various facts which would ensure its commercial success; among them was the disclosure that there was major traffic on the River Teign amounting to almost 10,000 tons annually; this included coal, culm, timber and corn as well as clay, much of which was confidentially expected to transfer to rail. A public meeting was held at the Castle Hotel in Dartmouth in November 1844 at which a resolution was carried supporting 'a Railway communication between the South Devon Railway and Torquay, Paingnton [sic], Torbay, Brixham and Dartmouth' - this appears to have been a rival scheme to the Torquay and Newton!

1845 was the year that 'railway mania' really came to Devon. As well as those outlined below there were other Companies 'provisionally registered' that year, they included: the **Plymouth Great Western Dock**, the **Direct Plymouth and Bideford Railway**, the **North Devon Railway**, the **Taw Vale Railway Extension and Dock**, the **Bridgwater and Minehead Junction Railway** ('uniting the Bristol and English Channels') and the **Great European Railway**.

Nearer home in September 1845 the **Dartmouth, Brixham, Torbay, Exeter & North Devon Junction Railway** plans were deposited. The prospectus explained it would 'authorise the construction and maintenance of a railway from Hoodown Farm [at Kingswear] ...to the township of Crediton with branches therefrom.' An interesting document of this stillborn adventure has survived.[11] A schedule asked for 'assent', 'dissent' or 'neutrality' as to whether land including 'the slip or hard of the Floating Bridge' should be acquired. When the railway actually came to Kingswear nearly 20 years later the problems were much the same. The Junction Railway was intended to follow the course of the Teign past Moretonhampstead where it would link with

16

the proposed **Cornwall & Devon Central Railway** also announced in 1845. The prospectus explained that it would be a 'Main Trunk line with good locomotive gradients' which would take its rails through Crediton and Okehampton to Camelford and Truro and finally on to Falmouth. At Truro there would be an extension line through West Cornwall to Penzance. At Exeter it would join with the standard-gauge line to London via Yeovil and Salisbury. The engineer was to be Joseph Locke. Locke was the London & South Western's engineer, and supported by some share-holders, determined to build a direct line from Basingstoke to the west to Exeter. The rivalry between this Company and the Great Western will be dealt with more fully in Chapter 7 so it is sufficient here to say that an Agreement was signed in January 1845 which aimed to reduce competition between them. It was only the first of a series, most soon broken and often flouted, which were to be made over the next 80 years. To further his ambitions Joseph Locke bought the manor of Honiton, and a seat for the town in Parliament. He served it, and most certainly his own interests, for 13 years!

A prospectus was also issued for the **Direct Exeter, Plymouth & Devonport Railway Company**. This stated that its line 'will commence at Exeter station of the proposed Yeovil and Dorchester line and proceed direct to Chudleigh where it will join with the 'Brixham & Torbay line', thus opening direct communication with Newton, Torquay, Paignton and Brixham. From the Teign it will proceed over Bovey Heathfield near the Potteries, passing the Rail of the Haytor Granite Works to Ashburton and Buckfastleigh where it is expected to meet the proposed Totnes, Buckfastleigh & Ashburton Railway. The engineering difficulties which have beset the South Devon atmospheric line are confirmed by daily experience, and thus render more necessary this direct communication'. This, like the Devon Central, although not stated, was standard-gauge as it promised 'direct access to the Royal Arsenal and Ports of Plymouth and Portsmouth from the Metropolis'. The company was said to be applying to Parliament in the current session but this was wishful-thinking. As will be seen the South Devon's problems referred to in this prospectus had only just begun, the worst was yet to come!

A serious attempt was also made to link Ashburton with Newton Abbot at the SDR Station there. In July 1845 a meeting at the Globe Hotel was told of the intentions of the **Ashburton, Newton & South Devon Junction Railway Company** to link the two towns.[12] Royal assent was obtained in July 1846 for the broad gauge line of ten and a half miles. No work was ever done and the Act lapsed five years later. The support outside the immediate area must have been in doubt in view of a statement made in February 1849 that 'there is a probability that the Ashburton Railway will be proceeded with, in order to open a second line from Newton to Marley Tunnel, which would not only open up a valuable branch, but would greatly facilitate the working of the main line, and prevent the chance of collision. It would afford a most desirable access to Holne Chase and other parts of the Moor from this neighbourhood'.[13]

Railway mania was also said to be the reason why the Dartmoor Investment Company with a required capital of £200,000 was formed 'for converting the wild wastes of Dartmoor into valuable arable and pasture land'. Fortunately the whole affair was soon forgotten.[14]

Between Dawlish and Teignmouth, early 1850s

In Torquay the imminent arrival of the railway, or so it is seemed then, caused trouble among two gentlemen and neighbours. A series of letters [15], one headed *South Devon Railway*, were written by and to Robert Dymond which indicate that C.H.Mallock (of Cockington) and Lord Sinclair of Pilmuir were both unhappy with the route of the line which the South Devon Railway was then proposing. They both wanted it to run as far to the north-east of the Turnpike road (which had been built from the Newton to Torquay Road through the Abbey meadows towards Paignton) as possible and not over their land. The Dartmouth Railway Co [that is the Junction Railway] proposal was also disliked. Mr Brunel however had made an arrangement with Mr Cary of Torre Abbey for a route through the meadows to the east of Chelston, land which did not belong to him but to the Mallocks! Mallock wrote with irritation: 'As far as the Tor Abbey Family making terms where the line should pass through our property, such an idea never occurred to me. I always understood that every possible opposition would be offered in that Quarter to any line of the Railroad. If you recollect what took place a few years since about the Coast road in front of Tor Abbey'.

The effect of the agreement was that the railway's route went through 15 chains of Mallock land compared with only a few hundred yards of Cary's! Mallock writes in one letter: 'My father employed one of the most eminent men in the Kingdom [Repton] to survey the ground and give him plans for building on it. The proposed line is marked in red and passes through some of the best building situations and will totally disrange the whole of the plans. Probably you are aware of the high terms on which ground for building now lets in Torquay for building purposes'. He also points out in another letter that the original survey was 'made without consulting us on the matter' and he preferred 'the Rival line' anyway.

In a later letter dated 28 March Mallock clearly shows his dislike of the Carys, writing 'although not on visiting terms with the present occupants of Tor Abbey I have not [forgotten] my old friendly recollections of the place and the Cary family that I shall regret if I am driven to do that which may annoy any member of the family ...' Possibly there were other reasons for this apparent animosity, the

Carys had been Catholics for centuries while the Mallocks were staunch members of the Established Church - and on occasions provided the incumbent at the parish church.

The 'Rival line' of the letter was of course the Torquay and Newton Railway company referred to above. In the event none of the schemes came to fruition and the South Devon Railway came only to the outskirts of Torquay.

Newton Station, about 1848; Torquay lines on right

II   EXETER TO PLYMOUTH

The Atmospheric Caper which failed

Much has been said and written in the last century and a half of Brunel's gross error in adopting the Samuda propulsion system using atmospheric pressure to power his trains west of Exeter. It is however only recently that a practical assessment has been possible. In 1981 the former Starcross pumping station, the only one surviving of those which worked the system, was purchased, albeit in a ruinous condition, and gradually an exhibition of memorabilia and other items is being created there.[1] The owner has however created a half-size working model, on which it is possible for up to three people to ride (powered in 1986 only by domestic vacuum cleaners) which shows that the system has two outstanding advantages; on the carriage the movement is silent and the acceleration smooth and rapid. Even the use of modern plastics has not completely solved the problems of the 'continuous valve' which was a vital part of the method.

Briefly, and there are several fuller accounts elsewhere[2], a cast-iron pipe or tube was laid between the rails which had a 2½ inch wide slot along it, with a leather valve or flap which sealed it along its whole length. A piston, attached to a carriage, or engine (which was of course coupled to the train) was placed in the end; air was then extracted from the pipe and the piston, and thus the train, was pulled to the end of the pipe, the valve opening in front of, and closing behind, the plate joining the piston to the carriage. Because it was the air at atmospheric pressure re-entering the pipe behind the piston which caused the forward motion it was described as an 'atmospheric system'. (The principle was used for many years on a smaller scale in large

21

*Photograph of Dawlish atmospheric chimney & house, early 1850s
(From a rare stereo-print)*

*'Brunel's Tower': the former atmospheric pumping station at Longpark,
Torquay. (Now a fruit warehouse; photographed 1987).*

department stores and national newspaper offices for conveying cash and messages around the buildings). On the South Devon the sections were about three miles long - the distance between the pumping stations, which were built beside the line, being about three miles. This short description gives little hint of the many practical problems encountered; for instance, initially three different size tubes were envisaged, depending on the task in hand (larger ones for gradients, etc.) so the piston had to be made adjustable to work in all three. Actually only ones of 15 inch diameter came into use between Exeter and Newton. At junctions the continuous tube had to be 'broken' so that the piston did not foul the rails; as there had to be no loss of pressure this was achieved by building subsidiary by-pass tubes below the rails: as the train was moving self-acting valves were invented to close the ends. These valves were also used at the engine houses so that the pumping arrangements could be changed to meet a situation, such as pumping simultaneously from sections on either side of it. Another problem, successfully overcome, was that minor distortions which occurred during casting the pipes, became magnified when they were laid end to end! The stationary engines were subjected to alterations and redesigns too.[3]

Among the major works done during the construction from Exeter to Newton was a timber bridge over the Exe; the river wall on the west bank of the River; the creation of the sea wall and permanent way between Dawlish Warren and Teignmouth (this involved the removal of vast quantities of the rock face as well) and the cutting of six tunnels between Dawlish and Teignmouth. Five of those tunnels: Kennaway, Coryton, Phillot, Clerk's and Parson's, are still there but the one at East Teignmouth was cut away when the line was doubled in stages between 1879 and 1884. The high lattice steel bridge with stone supports replaced it. The South Devon's headquarters was built in 1846 at street level below St. Thomas station. The facade of this building facing the City has been refurbished as part of the Plaza/ Sainsbury development to something approaching its original appearance and is now a restaurant. Parts of Brunel's 64-arch viaduct can still be glimpsed above the car-parking area there.

Work went on throughout the winter of 1844-45 and by February good progress had been made. Away from the sea coast much had been achieved but, as if a warning, there had been persistent easterly gales which had delayed the building of the sea-wall. The decision to land the stone from the sea in skips had not helped. The target date for completion was June 1845 but because of these and the problems with the 'bottomless' Cockwood Marsh, trains were to start running nearly 12 months late. Eventually the idea of an embankment there was abandoned and a Brunel-designed viaduct was put up instead. That viaduct was finally replaced in 1898-9 with an embankment but then the rider was added 'there are no signs of it giving way under the weight'. The story has also persisted that Dawlish station was designed by the great man himself on the back of an envelope.

It was decided not to wait for the completion of the atmospheric but to operate initially with steam engines. Two were hired from the GWR at a cost of 1/4d (7p) a mile and appropriately renamed *Exe* and *Teign*. On Whit-Saturday 1846 the first train left that City at 12.25 pm for Teignmouth, pulled by *Teign* hauling nine carriages. Crowds gathered at every possible vantage point and there were banners and a band when it arrived at Teignmouth - a form of celebration which was to be repeated many times over the next two decades. The return journey in the afternoon took just 38 minutes. On Whit-Monday the travellers exceeded all expectations; the morning down train somehow managed to convey 1500 passengers in the 21 carriages on the train - with almost an equal number squeezing on to the corresponding up train. The age of the train had arrived in South Devon.

In modern day parlance 'compulsory purchase powers' were necessary before the railway could be completed to Newton. Parliamentary approval had to be obtained for the final parcel of land and little was done in the way of heavy works over the Teign or Canal until this had been done and the route of the line assured. However, all went well and the works were ready for traffic by December. The first test train entered Newton drawn by two locomotives hauling a large number of loaded trucks weighing altogether nearly 400 tons. There was some surprise that bridges and embankments had survived such a load without collapsing. After the formal survey by the Government Inspector the line opened for passenger traffic on 31 December. The

Dawlish after the completion of 'Mr Brunel's bold and daring plan', c.1890

9.55 am train took just 55 minutes for the journey - on this occasion it was hauled by the locomotive *Antelope* as the atmospheric system was still not ready.

This opening took place with little public ceremony from the Newton people. Some years later *A trip on the South Devon Railway* appeared in local guidebooks.[4] Little is made of the town except to say that 'at this station passengers going to Torquay, Paignton, or Brixham change carriages [and] here also passengers for Ashburton quit the train, it being the nearest point, about seven miles, from that place'. In spite of the routing of the line west rather than east of Forde House the Newton people still felt their station was 'out of town.'

The Guidebook writer also has this to say about Dawlish:

Much was said during the progress of the railway of the great injury likely to be sustained by this delightful watering place, in consequence of its [the railway] passing between the beach and

25

the town. Mr Brunel's bold and daring undertaking received anything but benedictions. A moment's thought ought to have convinced any unprejudiced person that as the object of the Railway Company is to obtain as much traffic as possible, it was clearly in their interest to render Dawlish as attractive as they could, and to preserve rather than injure its character as a watering place.

Any comment seems irrelevant.

The revolution in rail transport, once it started, moved quickly. Cecil Torr, that gentle 'small-talker' from Wreyland near Lustleigh, relates how his father took 21 hours in the *Defiance* from Piccadilly to Exeter in 1841; just five years later on the Express it took six-and-a-half hours. Within a year he was able to come within a few miles of home at Newton Abbot. The cost was about £3.10s. by coach plus tips; by train it was £2.4s.6d First Class and £2.10s. on the express - and no tips at all. Rail was therefore the inevitable winner and accounts for the immediate decline of the old form of transport.

Trains between Exeter and Newton continued to be steam-hauled for the first eight months of 1847, then early in September a daily goods train was transferred to atmospheric working. A little later, in the middle of the month, the public were able to try it for themselves as passengers when two trains a day in each direction started operating. Over the next months the remainder were gradually transferred from steam so that by the end of February 1848 the whole line was 'atmospheric'. Even before this time questions were being asked about the efficiency of the system - in December 1847 the *Torquay Directory* had reported: 'A general meeting of the shareholders in the SDR will shortly be held in Exeter to consider the expediency of giving another trial to the atmospheric ... before finally abandoning it and incurring a further outlay to render the line fit for locomotives.' At the next half-yearly meeting the directors were however able to reassure the doubters and even confidently predict: 'the atmospheric apparatus has been completed and brought into active operation. I think we are in fair way of shortly overcoming the mechanical defects, and bringing the whole apparatus into regular and practical working, and as soon as we can obtain good and efficient communication between the Engine

Early days on the SDR: a train crosses the Teign near Newton Abbot

houses and thus ensure proper regularity in the working of the engines, we shall be enabled to test the economy of working'.

During that winter and spring which followed the problems which beset the Exeter to Newton line were monumental. Valves and joints in the tube gave trouble, the pumping stations suffered breakdowns, and there were troubles with the alignment of the continuous pipe.[5] The major problem concerned the sealing compound; initially a lime soap was used but this formed a hard skin on exposure to light and air so a more viscous mixture of soap and cod-oil was tried. In winter the leather valve froze solid too. By early summer it was realised the whole length of the valve leather needed replacing. In June steam engines took over; however the report of the Special Committee which reached the decision only recommended 'the suspension of the Atmospheric system until it should be made more efficient at the expense of the patentees and Mr Samuda'. The recurring story that it was rats which caused its demise may only be a legend. Undoubtedly they would have sought out the cod-oil and the rush of air through the pipe before the passing of the first train of the day probably brought some corpses among the other debris which ended up at the base of the pumping machinery in the engine houses.

Conditions inside the engine houses must have been rather horrific. As well as being hot and dusty, there must have been faults in the engines. In May 1848 William Wreyford was injured when 'the D valve fell on his foot'. His leg was later amputated in the Devon & Exeter Hospital. Even more intriguing is the report only a fortnight later that 'another man [were there others?] has been run over by a train between Dawlish and Starcross, he is supposed to have fallen asleep whilst employed in greasing the Atmospheric valve'.

In May the engine house at Dainton between Newton and Totnes was complete but it was never to be used. The August meeting of the Company at the Royal Hotel in Plymouth was given the bad news; the financial situation was 'most unsatisfactory, no profit had been made during the half-year; on the contrary there had been a loss of £2,500. The payment of the October dividend was therefore necessarily postponed. Losses were solely attributed to the Atmospheric system the cost of coals alone being 1/3d a mile more the whole expense of working the Midland line by locomotives; the whole outlay had amounted to upwards of £300,000'. So early in September suspension became abandonment - the 'Atmospheric Caper' was over. Some optimists however never stopped hoping; only a few days before this a new and improved *rubber* valve was being fitted at Dawlish. Later the *Torquay Directory*, quoting the *Railway Record*, optimistically said: 'Since the abandonment of the atmospheric system the returns on the South Devon line have been sufficient not only to cover the Debentures but to leave several thousands for interest on the six per cent preference shares'. However interest was not paid; in fact the Company's finances remained in a parlous state for some time and at one stage its survival seemed in doubt.[6]

Strangely reminiscent of the problems being encountered by the railways over a century later was the announcement in November that 'the Directors have resolved to reduce the salaries of the men on the line; policemen and porters to 14/- a week instead of 15/-, those of

Early days on the SDR: Newton Station built on the edge of town (Note the atmospheric pumping station in right hand corner)

higher grade will be reduced by 20 per cent. A great number of hands have recently been discharged all along the line and a further reduction in the number of porters, policemen and clerks is contemplated'. At the same time sale notices were issued for '680 tons of atmospheric railway tube each weighing about 8 cwt, lying at Bristol', together with other pig-iron. Much later, on 3 September 1855 there was a major sale of building materials at the 'Teignmouth and Summer-house engine houses'[7]: the latter was 'about mid-way between Newton & Teignmouth'. (Full list in *Appendix I*)

Some statistics have survived which show the potentialities of the system; by March 1848 '884 atmospheric trains had run: of which 790 had completed their journeys within the prescribed time'. This means little of course if the timings were excessively generous as they possibly were. The highest speed achieved seems to have been 68 miles per hour though working speeds were much lower. However, to the local people this must have seemed like flying; in 1851 a local omnibus owner was fined for exceeding 4 mph without a stage-carriage licence - an indication of the situation on the roads which was all they had ever seen before the railway came. One Brunel biographer wrote many years ago: 'Except when occasional mishaps caused delay, the new mode of traction was almost universally approved of. The motion of the train, relieved of the impulsive action of the locomotive, was singularly smooth and agreeable; and the passengers were freed from the annoyance of coke dust and the sulphurous smell from the engine chimney'. A visit to the Starcross replica will illustrate just how silent and smooth the operation could be! Apart from the Starcross engine house, two others survive: at Longpark near Torquay (now a fruit wholesaler's premises), which was never in operation but which has probably changed in appearance the least; and at Totnes where Unigate has incorporated the nineteenth century building into its dairy and creamery.

Keeping the Line by the Sea at Work.
The demise of the Atmospheric did not end the South Devon's problems on the coastal part of its line; almost as soon as it was completed along the edge of the sea between Dawlish Warren and Teignmouth, facing as it did, and still does, the full force of easterly gales, the cliffs and walls gave trouble. The first major fall was in 1853 when there was a landslip near Dawlish, caused by heavy rains rather than the sea[8]:

> During the last week there was an immense slip or fall near Holcombe Tunnel. Before the rails could be cleared, passengers and luggage were conveyed over the Turnpike road. All vehicles and horses which could be procured were put into requisition for this service and there was for a day or two a revival of old-fashioned modes of travel to the satisfaction of the old turnpike-gatehouse keepers. Some odd incidents arose in consequence, one good lady was indignant at being obliged to put up with an old country cart, but on the guard demanding a sight of her ticket, it was found to be a Parliamentary one which settled the matter.

There was a major breach of the wall two years later in 1855 when part of the wall and line were washed away between Dawlish and Teignmouth where 'the train has been consequently impeded and passengers obliged to alight and carry their luggage some distance ... The scene although a melancholy one, has a picturesque appearance, particularly at night-time when many workmen are employed and work by firelight while the raging sea is threatening them with destruction'.[9]

There was a great storm in October 1859 which did more damage on land than the Great Hurricane of 1866 when many ships and lives were lost at sea in South Devon. This time considerable damage was done to the track on both sides of Dawlish station '... the 5 o'clock train arrived at Dawlish but was unable to proceed; many passengers stayed inside throughout the night while others took refuge in hotels in the town' - a nightmare experience for the former. It was following this event that the wall east of Dawlish was substantially rebuilt.[10] Before the South Devon's demise they had one more storm to contend with; yet more damage was done in 1869 by a combination of spring tides and 'gales of immense violence'.

The 'Roller-Coaster' Road from Newton to Plymouth

The construction from Newton to Totnes was delayed everywhere by bad weather and there was much labour needed to tunnel out at Dainton, so it was not until 20 July 1847 that the single line opened with all the pomp and ceremony to be expected at such an ancient town! There was relief too in Brunel's eyes. Because power was to be 'atmospheric' the gradients (1 in 57 and 1 in 36) had been engineered more steeply than they otherwise would have been; thus when it became obvious that it would be steam, there were grave doubts as to whether the locomotives of the day would ascend them.

There were even more engineering problems to be overcome on the last 24 miles to Plymouth, which the Company determined to finish and open at one time. First there was a long, low viaduct at Rattery to build, then the half-mile tunnel at Marley Head to be dug out. The deep valleys of the Dartmoor rivers and streams necessitated high viaducts, which, because of his now limited financial resources follow-

31

Wooden viaducts between Totnes and Plymouth, engraved about 1850

ing the atmospheric fiasco, Brunel was forced to build five of these of wood (this included the one at Ivybridge, later replaced with a stone structure beside it). Lastly there was a steep gradient at Hemerdon which rose 273 feet in two miles on its west side. (It still exists and the occasional steam 'specials' are forced to slow dramatically). The South Devon, when it did finally arrive on 5 May 1848, was only to a temporary station at Laira Green. The Company continued to have problems with the Plymouth and Dartmoor Railway and with the Authorities so that it was not until 2 April 1849 that the public opening in Plymouth took place.[11] Brent, Wrangaton, Ivybridge and Plympton all opened on the same day (5 April 1848). As will be seen later they all, except Brent, closed on the same day too.

Initially there were six trains a day each way between Plymouth and Exeter; however much of the track was single, and any heavy traffic, particularly in summer, caused frustration, delays and general chaos. The laying of a second was therefore urgent and so a start was made in the 1850s - however it was over 50 years before the last section, between Dawlish and Teignmouth, went!

There was still another new railway to come. The first Kingsbridge and Salcombe Railway Act received Royal Assent in 1864 and its building started with the laying of the foundation stone of a bridge.[12] However the whole undertaking was abandoned in 1871 after much work, in places, had been done and Kingsbridge had to remain without a railway for 20 years longer! When work did finally restart it was carried out by the Great Western Railway. In the meantime, following representations from the Kingsbridge folk, Wrangaton was renamed *Kingsbridge Road*. It became *Wrangaton* again when the Kingsbridge branch opened to Brent in 1895.

It was however much earlier than this – and before the atmospheric disaster – that the South Devon Company was looking to another fast-growing group for additional income – the invalids of Torquay.

III THE RAILWAY REACHES TORQUAY

Trains to Torquay for Christmas.

The legislation which authorised the building of the railway from Newton to Torquay was rather cumbersomely called the South Devon Railway (Amendments & Branches) Act which received Royal Assent on 14 August 1846 and sanctioned the construction only as far as Tor (now more usually spelt Torre). It was explained:

> The remainder of the proposed line has been rejected in conseqence of petitions from owners of land in Paignton on the grounds that the gradients are incorrectly stated: the real objection being that the beach at both Paignton and Goodrington would have been rendered less accessible and the line would injure the property through which it passed ... The line to Dartmouth would be most expensive in construction and the least remunerative. [My italics] *There is little prospect of it ever being taken up either by the South Devon or by an independent company.* The South Devon may congratulate themselves on a fortunate defeat.

It is clear that local landowners had considerable influence on the course of events; they were said to be in favour of 'placing a terminus under Chapel Hill' but 'if it had not been for the opposition Pilmuir, Tor Abbey and Cockington would have been at the mercy of the South Devon directors and the extension to Dartmouth would have left Torquay in the background'. Within a fortnight it was reported that the contract for constructing the line had been given to Mr Richard Sharp who 'has acquired some celebrity for the rapidity with which his works have been executed'. The labourers, with their families, were moving in to annoy the gentry already crowding the streets of the growing town. At Totnes their living-conditions were diabolical – and the local tradesmen fleeced them as well[1]. When they were drunk they were impossible. There is no reason to believe they fared any better during the Torquay branch construction though no record survives. However their situation ten years later was little improved.[2] One sequel was the appearance in Paignton Petty Sessions court of a widow who sought 'to affiliate an illegitimate male child on a railway laborer, now working at Saltash'. The case was adjourned for the production of corroborative evidence!

In November there was a report that 'surveyors are actively engaged in surveying levels for an extension into Torquay. The most practicable seems to be a tunnel from Chapel Hill into the valley below the new Church [St Mary Magdelene, Upton] and then through the Back Lane to the Quay'. A few days later the South Devon was reported to be applying for an Act 'to make and maintain a railway commencing at or near the terminus of the railway ... to Torquay terminating at or near Morgan's Horticultural Establishment [Castle Circus] and also for an extension [to a site] near the market house on or near the Quay in the town and parish of Brixham'. Whilst nothing came of this suggestion either then or later (alternative schemes continued to be made from time to time), the effect of having a main terminus in the centre of Torquay in the narrow valley between the Castle and Waldon hills would have made a fundamental difference to the way Torquay, and possibly the rest of Torbay, developed. There was a more immediate problem. In these days the health of the community is taken for granted but little more than a hundred years ago there were frequent outbreaks of the cholera – and South Devon was not immune. A local doctor commenting on the 1849 epidemic just a year later 'blamed' the railway for possible future occurrences; he said:

When the South Devon Railway was first projected it was proposed to bring this line into the town. In this case the terminus would have been in Swan Street [near the harbour and now an area still requiring urgent and expensive redevelopment], and all the houses would have been pulled down to have provided the large open space for the offices of the Company, unfortunately this portion of the scheme was opposed by the inhabitants, and Swan Street remains to give an ever ready reception for fresh visits from this and other epidemics.

As has been seen in the previous chapter the Company was in dire straits by the end of 1848 but in September it was announced that: 'The line is ballasted throughout and the permanent rails are laid at the Newton extremity. Mr Harrison, mechanic of the works is shortly to resign in favour of Mr Darley, the resident engineer, a pupil of Mr Brunel'. A month later 'the permanent rails are laid as far as Kingskerswell and have been traversed by the engines conveying materials for the remainder of the line'. Announcing the forthcoming opening the Torquay Directory said: 'Nor will the festivities be confined to the rich

For whilst they feted all the great
They ne'er forgot the small'.

All classes of people were catered for. On 18 December the first train arrived at Torquay [Tor] Station, incidentally more than three months earlier than it did at Plymouth, headed by GWR's 2-4-0 *Taurus*, which was decorated with evergreens and flags. There were nine First class and 15 Second Class carriages; the journey time was 13 minutes. There was a great procession comprising: outriders with flags; Torquay Temperance Band; Town Commissioners; the Gentlemen and Tradesmen of Torquay; Teignmouth Temperance Band, and 'the new busses from the Royal and Family Hotels with their four blacks and four greys.' The whole population turned out in holiday attire. The speeches showed great optimism for the future and there was sympathy for 'Pratt and the other old coachmen whom steam had put off the road'. Torquay must become the metropolis of Torbay, said Sir John Yarde Buller. The first business of the day was a distribution of bread and meat to the poor, a pound of each being given to every member of their families. Tickets had been granted on the preceding days, at the Town Hall, to all those considered eligible, bearing the number of the booth in the Market Place where the provisions were to be shared out to them. (The population of Torquay was only about 10,000 then, and there had been bread riots in 1847). At half past ten the procession began to form in the square between the Hotels; banners on show included salutations to 'Brunel and the Broad Gauge'. Brunel himself was one of the 200 passengers on the train. In the evening there was a grand dinner at the Royal Hotel. The participants were very much not of the working class.[3]

So important was the fish trade at Brixham that almost immediately the South Devon was considering extending the railway to Livermead to facilitate the landing of fish. The arrival of the railway meant that fresh fish could now be sent packed in ice, imported from the Arctic, to London and other large centres of population. One spectacular method was adopted by Mr Wintle of the London Inn at Brixham who kept large light spring waggonettes to which could be harnassed four fast carriage-horses. The fish was conveyed to Torre. Sometimes however the train had left but, not daunted, the driver, knowing the train must stop for at least half-an-hour at Newton, would push on to Teignmouth to await its arrival there. On a summer evening crowds used to wait by the Turnpike road at Livermead to see the vehicles race by.[4]

A glance at an early timetable shows the extent of the service which was:

8 15 am	'To Exeter'	1st, 2nd, 3rd
9.05 am	'Above Bristol'	1st, 2nd, 3rd
11.20 am	'Express'	1st, 2nd only
1.05 pm	'Mail'	1st, 2nd only
6.13 pm	'Above Tor'	1st, 2nd, 3rd
8.10 pm	–	1st, 2nd only

This last reached London at 4.50 am the next morning, a tremendous improvement on stage-coaches in both speed and comfort.

There was great activity when those early trains came in and went out. Hotel omnibuses, and others driven by enterprising private operators, congregated in the station yard. One of the latter can only be identified as 'Mr Wolfinden's omnibus'. His driver avoided paying the shilling toll at Tor Turnpike Gate when rushing for the one o'clock train – and landed up in court for doing so! Towns not served by the railway arranged to transport intending passengers to the nearest station; soon Mr Mills of Brixham was encouraging the Dartmouth people to make a journey. An advertisement in 1849 announced: 'The *Why not* omnibus leaves the Castle Hotel daily at 5.45 am and reaches Tor Station [not Torquay to the Dartmouthians] in time for the 8.15 am 1st, 2nd and 3rd class'. It returned after the arrival of the evening train and patrons were promised 'fares very low'.

The South Devon's plans for any further expansion ended when in February 1849 it was stated that at a Directors' meeting the extension past St Michaels [Tor Station] would be postponed until the prospects of the Company improved.

It will be noticed that third class passengers had to travel either early in the morning or in the evening. The Cheap Trains Act of 1844 had stipulated that '3rd Class passengers must be protected from the

GWR engine No 2170 Taurus
(From Brixham Museum's picture collection)

weather' so by about 1850 most of the open ones, like those seen in some early lithographs, had gone. The early Third Class carriages were designed simply so that passengers could not fall out, that is without windows, and with only small roof ventilators which could be opened in hot weather! The improvement of Third Class accommodation seems to have brought problems. In 1847 the South Devon directors reported to their shareholders that

> though they were desirous to hold out every encouragement to Third Class passengers, that might not interfere prejudicially with First and Second Class traffic, but the extent to which advantage of the accommodation thus afforded by classes of persons for whom it was not intended, has obliged your Directors, in opening the further portion to Totnes, to reduce the number of Third Class trains, and so to regulate the time they run, as to adapt them, as far as circumstances permit, to the wants of the working classes.[5]

Whether this affected the habits of travelling South Devonians is not known.

Almost as soon as the Torquay line started operating the demand for changes and improvements began. Early in 1849[6] a Memorial was sent to the Postmaster General: 'London bags arrive at Newton Station about 5 am from whence they are carried by mail cart to Torquay where they are due at 6 am. If the bags were brought by train they would gain 40 minutes. The risk and inconvenience of the mode of conveyance by a wretchedly horsed cart driven by a boy is a matter of still greater importance; the conveyance by the now unfrequented road taking place during the night'. Theft of the mails was a problem then too.

Two newspaper reports in the summer of 1850 tell graphically how quickly the lives of local people changed; the masses could now take a day out. In the first, headed *A Railway Ramble*, readers were warned that 'some enterprising individual in Exeter has engaged a holiday train to visit Torquay on Monday next. Determined to do it cheaply, he has arranged for 500 Exonians to be taken 52 miles there and back for half a crown [12½p]. The train will leave at a quarter before seven and will be in Torquay in less than an hour. It will return at eight o'clock in the evening'. The next issue confirmed that the 'monster excursion train' had indeed arrived but with 806 tickets taken the town had 'literally swarmed with Exonians, who seemed resolved upon enjoying a full half-crown's worth of the beauty of Torquay's scenery'.

The coming of the railway clearly caused problems too for those towns and villages which had been by-passed. Kingskerswell was so desperate to have a station of its own that the inhabitants were quite prepared to build it themselves, but the Company were only agreeable to consent to the 'stoppage of one train a day'. They were 'much inconvenienced by the discontinuance of communication by stage coach or omnibus'; there were worries too of the 'danger of robbery during the approaching winter as the journey is made late in the evening and before daylight along a road which is now unfrequented'. How little people's concerns have changed in nearly a century and a half.

Visits to the 1851 Great Exhibition
The name of Thomas Latimer of the *Western Times* in Exeter and the part he played in encouraging the use of the railway by the people of Exeter has already been chronicled.[7] The Great Exhibition of 1851 was the first great event after the advent of the railway to catch the imagination of ordinary folk and draw them to London. Just as in Exeter clubs were formed throughout the County into which small amounts at a time could be paid; at Dawlish one was 'formed by the book-keeper of the London Inn for enabling of members to visit the Great Exhibition in Hyde Park; the fare to London and back will be about 16/- [80p] and it is expected that about 25 will avail themselves of the opportunity thus afforded them'. At Torquay an excursion train set off in July with 'subscribers to the Penny Bank fund' totalling 80 people. This proved so popular that a further train was put on to run on 2 August when many members of Exeter and other Temperance societies were expected to go too.

St Marychurch was then independent of its larger neighbour and it lays claim to Isambard Kingdom Brunel as their 'squire' after he purchased his estate at Watcombe. Although Brunel laid out the

Isambard Kingdom Brunel

grounds and designed a mansion the property known as Brunel Manor, owes nothing to the great man himself. Death overtook him in September 1859 before he was able to lay one stone of his dream-house. Typical of the man was his generosity at the time of the Exhibition; the *Torquay Directory* tells how his estate labourers left Tor station early on the 13 August for London. 'They occupied the bodies of two carriages and started in high spirits. Met by a guide at Paddington they went to the Chrystal [sic] Palace, the Thames Tunnel, and the British Museum'. The party went on Tuesday and returned on Saturday. 'The whole of their expenses were defrayed by their kind employer, and their weekly wages paid as if they had continued at work'.

It is unexpected to find that one sedate little Victorian town attracted attention countrywide so early as it did. In September 1851 the *Scotch Reformers Gazette* featured a long article on Torquay:

> It presents a most captivating appearance to a stranger; and the excellence of its accommodation for all classes of invalids, bid fair to make it the best frequented watering-place in the kingdom. From Glasgow and Edinburgh transit is easy, and by railway all the way. Leaving Glasgow at 12; by mail train to Birmingham and going straight on by Gloster and Bristol the traveller reaches Torquay the next day at the same hour.

The First Accident, Boxing Day 1851

In reality journeys were not always quite so uneventful as this; what appears to have been the first serious mishap on the 'Torquay branch' took place on 26 December 1851 when:

> Passing Low's Bridge the steam was shut off as usual, the train descending the incline by its own gravity ... A passenger assures us that he distinctly heard the signal calling for 'breaks' twice but the motion increased rather than decreased ... It swept by the station at a speed that rendered it all but certain it would be carried over the slopes by which the line terminates. Several passengers tried to leave the carriages but without success as the doors were locked and the imprisoned passengers were hurried on in the dark to what seemed certain destruction; we believe there were no lights in either of the carriages ... The engine

finished up at the bottom of the slope [now Avenue Road towards the sea front] with the Third Class carriage halfway down. Fortunately no one was badly injured.[8]

Having recorded the graphic details, that un-named Victorian journalist added an observation of his own which no doubt summed up the fears of his contemporaries: 'it has been suggested that that part of the line which extends beyond the station should ASCEND a steep gradient, so that an unmanageable train, if such things there must be, might be stopped by the aclivity'.

The 1840s and 1850s were the most progressive decades in the growth of Torquay: the population almost doubled in the first and in the second, perhaps the greatest days, it was attracting visitors 'of the highest class'. Private enterprise, perhaps with them in mind, quickly discovered the importance of the guidebook for publicity purposes and so a succession appeared extolling the town's virtues. In one published in 1851 there appears the short statement: 'It [the railway] has been found highly advantageous to the town as well as a great convenience to visitors. It is in contemplation to extend the railway through Torre Abbey lawn skirting the new road to a station near the coal cellars on the Western Quay'. The building of a new Torquay station on the Strand remained an obsession for some years.

Just about twelve months later there was a 'Public Meeting re the extension of the railway into Torquay'. The poster advertising this has survived and gives a list of all its supporters. Whilst the shop assistants were still putting in a day's work which started at 8 am and ended at 7.30 pm six days a week, one group of workers did warrant a mention, the ten 'flymen'. A fly was the small hackney carriage on which many of the residents and visitors relied for conveyance to and from their homes to the station. The meeting heard three schemes: 1 and 2 took curves of different radii which swept from the station towards the Bay passing in front of Torre Abbey: one was to use the Harbreck Rock, still visible at low water, for foundations. The third would have cut through the higher portion of Torre Abbey grounds by means of a deep cutting which would be arched over and filled in afterwards, traversing the New Road near the Toll-Bar to a direct line near the Quay. Mr

43

Hack (a local dignitary and magistrate), preferring a town centre route, reminded those present: 'It was first proposed the line should touch Swan Street and George Street and I would be glad to see it carried out as it would confer a great benefit in getting rid of that intolerable seat of disease'.

This illustrates several aspects of the situation in mid-Victorian times. The 'New Road' is of course Torbay Road and is a good example of how many seaside places acted when faced with a land crisis; a wall was built on the beach and the space behind filled in - the railway line would be added on the sea side using the same method. The 'Toll-Bar' was a stone-built house with the gate needed to collect the Turnpike Trust's dues - it is still there and is now a public convenience! Over the years a slum had grown up in the lower part of the town with sanitary conditions so bad that there had been an outbreak of the cholera, referred to earlier, which had killed 66 people only three years before. There was general support for an extension though a rival group, at another venue, demanded that matters should remain as they were.

A Bill was presented to the next Session of Parliament and although little or no opposition was expected it did not complete its stages and there were no further plans until two years later, when two public meetings were held in support of the Torquay and South Devon Railway Extension Company Bill which was later submitted to the 1854 Session. This proposed 'making a Railway from the Pier or Harbour of Torquay to the Torquay Branch of the South Devon Railway and a Branch to a point near Livermead House'. The local Board of Health submitted a petition in support which said that [inter-alia] 'an unusual proportion of the inhabitants consist of gentry, many of whom are invalids, resorting to Torquay for the sake of the climate [and] there is a turnpike intervening and some parts of the thoroughfares of Torquay are narrow and inconvenient and occasionally crowded with omnibuses and carriages'. It was withdrawn in April before an Admiralty Enquiry could take place. There were rival meetings at Brixham which petitioned against the Torquay extension and insisted that any new line should be carried to Livermead. This was finally done but it was not by the South Devon Railway Company.

IV ON TO KINGSWEAR: THE DARTMOUTH AND TORBAY RAILWAY COMPANY

Not a year went by without some new scheme or extension to the South Devon being promoted. In August 1853 work started doubling the lines from Newton towards Plymouth, the Torquay line being used as far as Aller. First however it is necessary to explain the unusual layout of the stations of the day. The UP and DOWN stations were not opposite each other but side by side so the layout of the tracks looked rather like a 'spaghetti junction' with rails. This was neatly summed up by William Winget: 'I well remember that on several occasions my father and I walked from Paignton to Torre Station to take the train for Dawlish and Exeter. At Newton there were then two stations, one for up traffic, another for down; so that if you were going Exeter way you went to one station, if going Plymouth way you went to another'. There were in fact three stations because when the Torquay branch was inaugurated a separate line including a covered platform had been built. Newton was rebuilt as a two-sided junction station between 1859 and 1861; the locomotive sheds were enlarged at the same time. A local paper reported that 'the works are becoming of such magnitude and employing such a number of skilled workers and housing is so difficult that the South Devon Railway have determined to erect 150 houses for their employees'. When viewing problems today it is often forgotten that no major social changes have taken place without a surge in demand for property.

Even more important to those parts of South Devon still without a railway, 1853 saw the issue of the prospectus of the **Dartmouth Railway Company** (also called the **Dartmouth, Torquay & South**

45

Devon). This may have been a successor to the **Torquay, Brixham and Dartmouth Railway Company** which in November 1852 had been unable to submit its Bill to Parliament as 'Mr Brunel had advised them to postpone it as he had not had sufficient time to prepare the plans' – but nothing more is known of it. The sponsors of the new Dartmouth Company included the Great Western, the Bristol & Exeter and the South Devon; important residents involved included Lord Courtenay among others. The Committee of Management was to be under the

'*Cutting the first sod*' *at Torre, January 1858*
(Illustrated London News *engraving*)

chairmanship of John Belfield, Esq. of Paignton. The chief engineer was again to be Brunel. Among the reasons why the line would be successful was that 'the capabilites of the land-locked harbour at Dartmouth were laid before the public in the Report of a Government Commission in 1840 [and] ... it is also a place of embarkation for passengers and emigrants'. The prospectus did not explain that the Commission's recommendations had not been implemented – and indeed never were.

The route of the proposed railway was 11 miles in length and approached quite near to Brixham which was then becoming an important fishing port. Equally of interest is the prophecy of a future for Paignton 'in climate of equal salubrity with Torquay, it possesses, in addition, a hard sandy beach nearly two miles in length, admirably adapted for bathing. Being in the centre of the Bay, it also embraces, within easy drives, all points of beauty ... [it] annually draws to it numerous visitors for health as well as recreation'. Foresight indeed because then three vast stretches of marshland lay between those sands and undeveloped Preston, Paignton and Goodrington. The necessary finance was not forthcoming but interest was not allowed to die completely and a Public Meeting was held at the Guildhall, Dartmouth on 6 September 1856, resulting in the setting up of a Committee to 'personally inspect the country between Totnes and Dartmouth and between Torquay and Dartmouth, with a view of ascertaining if any less expensive Line could be made than the one proposed in 1853'. The printed Report it prepared contains detail which can be used as a social history of Victorian South Devon.[1] Traffic would come from Mails, Passengers and Merchandise. It continued:

> The Mails alone are a very important feature: besides Mr W S Lindsay's important Line of Mail Packets, which consist of one vessel departing and arriving every month, numerous Mails are landed here under the present disadvantages from Foreign Vessels, because this Port is so well situated for that purpose, when ships enter the English Channel with a contrary wind; and the Committee consider that by the time this Railway is open, many new lines of Mail Steam ships will be established, a fair proportion of which, with some of the present lines, will undoubtedly use this Harbour, when its great natural advantages will be demonstrated.

One ship a month providing substantial traffic was wishful-thinking and the arrival of steam-ships would soon make 'contrary winds in the Channel' irrelevant.

The proposed railway would do much to put the district on the map. The Committee promised: 'One great benefit of Mail Packets is that the majority of Passengers invariably land and embark with the Mails, to save the tedious channel voyage, and these will add considerably to the local passenger traffic, while at the same time persons coming from Foreign Lands, to reside in England, are landed in the mildest and most picturesque part of the Kingdom, [and thus] will at once be able to locate themselves in this healthy district'. Of passengers it was also confident:

> The population of the district to be benefitted may be taken at the lowest estimate of 30,000, and therefore productive of great local traffic, and also considering the numerous visitors and residents at Torquay, the increasing repute of Paington [sic] as a watering place, the great attractions of Dartmouth and vicinity, and the very large back country between Dartmouth and Kingsbridge, the Committee can confidently give their opinion that the number of Passengers will equal, if not exceed, those between Torquay, Newton, Teignmouth and Exeter.

The expected business traffic would be profitable too. As well as Brixham fish (100 tons was being sent by rail every week from Torquay), 'Paington and that district exports a large quantity of Cider, and with a Railway the cost will be lessened and the facilities so increased as much to enlarge that branch of traffic ... Other optimistic predictions included: 'The Fruit trade [of Salcombe] might also be made a source of profit [and] the Bordeaux, Spanish, and Portuguese Merchants would find this the nearest and best port for their merchandise, a large portion of which at present goes to Bristol; but this would considerably shorten the voyage and save the dangers of the Bristol Channel' Finally it thought that 'the exporters of clay around Newton, and the owners of the Potteries would also resort to this harbour, as ships could always be chartered here with advantage'. Perhaps not surprisingly after such an appraisal, the prospectus of the Dartmouth and Torbay Railway Company appeared in October. There was little difference from the 1853 prospectus except that the line was now only 7½ miles in length because it went only 'as far as the sixth milestone, and diverging hence above Galmpton village to go under Higher Greenway to Maypool or Noss'. The Directors were the most influential people in this part of the County and included: Charles Seale Hayne (the Agricultural College near Newton Abbot perpetuates the name); Lord Churston of Lupton; William Froude of Chelston Cross (who had built there the very first experimental ship-tank in the world) and J.F.Luttrell of Nethway (near Brixham but better known as the family at Dunster Castle in Somerset). William Winget, noted earlier, penned his memory of the group thus:

> The directors experienced many difficulties in the selection of a line which should not be too expensive and yet at the same time one that would meet the wishes of those who had become shareholders, the majority of whom had invested their money not expecting to receive immediate or direct profit, but hoping eventually to derive advantage from the increased value of the land and house property.

The Dartmouth and Torbay Railway Act received Royal Assent on 27 July 1857. The chief engineer was Mr Brunel assisted by Messrs Margary (the resident engineer of the SDR who lived at Dawlish) and Bell: the solicitors were Tozer, Whidborne, MacKenzie & Tozer of Teignmouth. Although the cuttings were to be sufficient for a double line of rails, as an economy, only a single broad-gauge line was to be laid in the first instance.

The grand ceremony of 'cutting the first sod' took place on 21 January 1858 below Torre Station by Sir L.V.Palk MP in a field about 500 yards from Torquay station where a large tent had been erected. It was witnessed by great numbers of people including the Mayor and Corporation of Dartmouth.[2] Mr Margary, the assistant engineer, handed Sir Lawrence a polished steel spade and a handsome mahogany wheel-barrow. He however proved an indifferent gardener, being incapable of getting the soil on his tool without bending down. Mr Seale Hayne on the other hand attacked his with such gusto that the spade snapped in half in his hands. The Rifle Brigade fired a *feu-de-joie*, the navvies shouted and the Brixham fishermen cheered ... More speeches were said, one speaker reminding the crowds that 'the sun, although it is only January, is shining upon us. I trust it might be the forerunner of the prosperity of Torquay, of Torbay, of Dartmouth, of the vicinity'. The proceedings ended when 'the Company then retired to the tent where "success to the Railway" was toasted in BUMPERS OF CHAMPAGNE which was supplied in profusion with suitable edibles. The procession then marched back to the Union Hotel where over 200 dined'.

There was some delay in commencing as not all the land at Torre had been acquired; not until March was it announced that 'a large quantity of train-waggons, rails, wheel-barrows and other necessary materials has arrived and a large range of stabling erected at Liver-mead. Large importations of "navvies" are now daily expected'. Work did not actually start until 20 May and it was while searching for this date in the *Torquay Directory* that the writer found details of a serious situation which had arisen among the large number of navvies working on the London and South Western's Honiton to Exeter line. Iniquitous conditions of work had forced them to take strike action. The chief cause of it was the truck system pursued by the 'gangers', which was not only illegal but also robbed the men of their hard-earned wages. The circumstances were told thus: 'Most of the gangers, whose duty it is to pay the men, supply them with provisions at exorbitant profits to themselves, and at the end of each month the accounts are made up and the men receive the balance'. The gangers had the power of dismissal and used this ruthlessly until the men could stand it no longer! Goods in lieu of cash in hand had been outlawed centuries earlier but the first 'modern' Truck Act of 1831 had made it unlawful – even then working men had some rights. Although there have been others since, the right of a workman to be paid in currency of the Realm is, at the time of writing, the same as that enjoyed by the navvies in the 1850s.

In June a Working Agreement was drawn up between the South Devon and the Dartmouth and Torbay. This document, written in immaculate copper-plate script, survives.[3] It shows that the latter would provide everything for the safe working of the line including sidings, passing places and electric telegraph. The SDR would provide engines, rolling stock, staff and all stores and materials.

By August 'progress had been made but the contractors had not been able to proceed with full force'. The embankment at Torre had been commenced while the cutting at Chelston was in a forward state. Shortly after the tunnel at Livermead (this was to remain there for nearly 50 years) was started and the bridge over the public carriageway at Chelston was under construction. The observant William Winget wrote many years later:

> I well remember the navvies and quarrymen working away at the tunnel under Livermead, for once a month I would distribute among them the *British Workman* and *Band of Hope*, with which the recipients were always well pleased. The necessary stabling, toolhouses, workshops, stores, etc ... were the five acres where the Recreation Ground now stands and I can picture when the ground was cleared for a move to a spot beyond Paignton, rats had found good quarters in the field where there had been so much corn and fodder for scores of horses, so a kind of *battue* was arranged. At the end of the hunt over 200 corpses were laid out on the ground, some as large as cats.

Clearly the ill-feeling of earlier years against the Railway Company had continued because in September a letter to Exeter reported that the Company's surveyor had been refused permission to go on to Lord Sinclair's land to make a map in connection with the latter's claim for compensation.[4] There were some successes in this struggle. A month later an Arbitration suit was agreed between the Railway and Matthew Churchward concerning land at Cockington. Various other arbitrations were settled soon after. Lord Sinclair of Pilmuir had claimed £18,000 for a bridge over his drive (now the driveway to the Rowcroft Hospice). In response the Company offered £250-500. The Arbitrator's award was £1200! At the same time Matthews, a lodging house owner, was awarded £515. Mr Mallock of Cockington took action in the Court of Chancery to stop the works totally. An Injunction was refused. This action was not finally withdrawn until April 1859.

In November a Memorial was sent to Lord Churston from the fishermen of Brixham requesting an extension of the railway to Old-Way. [This was not Oldway at Paignton but a locality just one mile from Brixham which had been by-passed by the revised route of the railway]. They explained that it was costing 6/- per cwt to send fish to London compared with only 2s.8d from Hull; they were suffering because the trade had become uncompetitive. Their appeal had no effect.

The Paignton Pudding.

The work proceeded apace and by July the line as far as Paignton was nearing completion – it was confidently expected that it would open on 21July 1859; the first engine however only got to Livermead on the 11th. The revised opening day of 1 August proved to be as spectacular an event as might be seen anywhere! It had been resolved to celebrate

CELEBRATION OF   THE OPENING

OF THE DARTMOUTH AND TORBAY RAILWAY, TO PAINGTON, AUG. 1st, 1859;

REVIVAL OF THE ANCIENT CHARTER OF

THE WONDERFUL PAINGTON PUDDING,
AND SOME PARTICULARS ABOUT IT.

THIS Pudding bore the form of a pyramid, and was gaily decorated. The ingredients were, 573 pounds of flour, 191 pounds of bread, 382 pounds of raisins, 191 pounds of currants, 382 pounds of suet, 95 pounds of sugar, 320 lemons, 144 nut-megs, and 360 quarts of milk, which made, in the aggregate, a total weight of two thousand one hundred pounds! The Pudding was made in sec-tions, and was built up on a waggon. The pro-cession was formed at Primley, the residence of John Belfield, esquire, at noon, from whence the cortege proceeded by way of Weston House, and through Winner-street, on by Matthews'-house, down by the Cross-road, and through Gerston-terrace to the Railway Station, and from thence to The Green, where about 3000 people of the parish of Paignton, as well as the brave men who made THE LINE, all seated in a circle, partook of THE FEAST! The Pudding was a ton weight, and drawn by eight horses, there were, also, four waggon loads of beef, bread, and cider. Excur-sion trains ran from all parts of the county, several steamers made trips, and Mr. Anthony Nicks, the harbour-master, threw open the harbour, free. The bells sent forth merry peals. Hundreds of pretty hats and bonnets graced the fair forms of the daughters of Paignton, and the young gentlemen of Torquay took good care to steel their hearts be-fore venturing on the green! Even the old men and women who partook of a like Pudding forty-two years ago were much exhilirated by the fun. A splendid band of music attended, and beaux and belles danced on the green, while the never-ceasing waves of the beautiful and glorious sea kept time.

ORDER
OF
THE PROCESSION.
—o—
Policemen.
Navies with picks & shovels.
Waiters.
Band.
Bread, in waggon with three horses.
Beef, in waggon with three horses.
Beef, in waggon with three horses.
Body of carvers.
Cider, in waggon with two horses.
Cider, in waggon with two horses.
Committee.
PUDDING!!
in waggon with eight horses.
Committee.
Secretary.
General
Arrangement Committee.
Policemen.
Inhabitants.

Policemen. Waiters with Flags. Policemen. Waiters with Flags.

Thousands of persons visited the scene of the fes-tivities, and the whole must have formed a lasting feature in the memory of the youngest inhabitant! A great number of those who walked to the feast at noon, got an attack of night-mare in the evening! No accident of great moment occurred, save that which happened to a certain young lady, whose cr noline was so large that the carvers when getting near the bottom of the pudding actually took pos-session of it to keep the pudding from tumbling to pieces—a wise precaution on their part, con-sidering the number of hungry boys from Torquay and Brixham who stood looking on with open mouths. So much for the utility of Crinoline!

But, as it is intended to say a word or two here about the beautiful sites for building, &c., at this delightful spot, I must now pass on. Paignton is about three miles from the pet-spot of Devon, Torquay, five from Brixham, five from Totnes, and eight from Dartmouth. It is situated in a remarkably rich and fertile district, and the sce-nery around it is very beautiful, consisting of wooded combes and gently rising hills, with the sea and the coast of Berry Head on one hand, and that approaching Portland on the other, to be seen from their summits. One of the great attractions of Paignton is its beautiful beach of smooth hard sand, which is nearly a mile in length. The ivy-covered ruins of a once magnificent palace are to be seen close to the church. Paignton is the second station of the Dartmouth and Torbay Railway. May PROSPERITY long attend it and THE PEOPLE OF PAINGTON !

PRINTED ON THE GREEN, AT PAINGTON, BY JOHN ROBINSON, OF TORQUAY.—PRICE ONE PENNY.

'Paignton Pudding' broadsheet, 1859

the day with the baking and distribution of the famous PAIGNTON PUDDING so a Committee of prominent Paigntonians was formed. John Robinson, a printer of broadsheets and tracts, set up his press on Paignton Green and printed a penny souvenir fully recording both the recipe and the sequence of the day's events.

What really happened was very different from those anticipated by Mr Robinson:

> The day of the opening dawned and invited to the event were the poor of Paignton, Marldon and Stoke Gabriel together with the navvies and their families who had worked on the extension of the line. Besides the Pudding there was 1900 lbs each of meat and bread and unlimited quantities of the local product, Devonshire cider. The procession left Primley at noon; prominent were the three wagons each drawn by three horses carrying the food and the great pudding on a wagon drawn by eight horses. After its safe arrival on Paignton Green the invited guests sat down inside the rope barrier while the rest of Paignton and neighbourhood pressed around on the outside. The meal proceeded peacefully until the pudding was drawn into position ready for cutting up; the people on the outside began to clamour for shares and, breaking down the fence, started forward to help themselves. The committee, worried by this turn of events, surrounded their charge and called on the FIVE POLICEMEN present to assist them. The invited guests, feeling that they were being deprived of their rights, moved into the fray and IN A MOMENT COMMITTEE, POLICE, PUDDING AND PUBLIC WERE IN ONE SEETHING MASS ON THE GROUND. By the time order was restored not a morsel of that delicious pudding remained ... It was said that there were over 18,000 people on the Green that day. The postmaster reported that greasy parcels were being sent off for the next few weeks.[5]

Although the distance was only 3 miles; there were 20 bridges, a viaduct and a tunnel (about 145 yards long at Hollacombe). The new Torquay station which had been erected on rising ground near Chelston (near the present New Grand Hotel) overlooking Torre Abbey Sands opened the same day as Paignton. From there the line crossed the viaduct behind Livermead House. Immediately there were complaints – Torquay station was only one third of the size of Torre and stood 'in the teeth of the East wind ... pulmonary invalids will say "This is a colder place than we came from"'. The timetable shows that up trains left Paignton at 7.15, 9.50, 11.15 am, 12.50 and 3.10 pm. The first train of the day included a 3rd Class carriage to all stations as far as Exeter. The 1848 Torquay Station became Torre and almost immediately there were representations that an alternative name should be found – unsuccessful attempts have continued on and off for nearly a hundred years.

The obsession to build a station on the Strand continued. Make-do-and-mend was the keynote of the next scheme. Three months after the line to Paignton opened, Parliamentary notice was given of the incorporation of a company to build a rail or tramway, drawn by horses, from the harbour to the new station. A Meeting at Webb's Hotel was told that Mr Errington had constructed tramways along public roads for about £1,200 a mile; he used old rails, stone sleepers and the part of the road between the rails was paved with stone. Nothing came of it and no plans have survived.

At the end of 1859 the Company reported that between 1 August and 31 December 78,853 passengers had been carried of whom 16,303 were to Paignton and 38,443 to Torquay. Later Mr J.T.White was to explain:

> By building a station at Livermead it partly satisfied Brixham's wishes but also every passenger who booked to Torquay would have to travel over the first mile of the Dartmouth and Torbay and thus provide an income which was in the long-term to save the Company from absolute bankruptcy.[6]

The original intention was to construct two wooden viaducts between Goodrington and Churston (in some respects a pity as Brunel-designed structures were so elegant) but it was decided to substitute masonry instead. This delayed their completion and gave the opportunity for those against the building of the line to the north bank of the Dart to submit a Bill to Parliament for a **Deviation**

Railway 'authorising the Dartmouth and Torbay Railway Company to abandon making a Portion of their authorised Line of Railway and make another Portion of Railway instead thereof, and to establish Steam Communication on the River Dart ... [by building] a new railway in or near a field in the parish of Churston Ferrers lying about 100 yards northward of the public highway ... and terminating at a point about 100 yards southwards of a pier or landing stage at Greenway ferry otherwise Dittisham ferry'. Section 23 gave the Company power to purchase or hire steam vessels for use between there and Dartmouth and any other places in or adjoining the River Dart.

It was pointed out that continuing on the approved route would be an expensive business: a tunnel and two viaducts would have to be built and other costs had risen above estimates. The amount required was now £80,000, partly because the landowners were demanding larger sums than those they had previously agreed to accept, and £2,000 had been paid to the owner of the Floating Bridge. It was also admitted that all the money originally subscribed had been spent and the directors were covering additional loans from their own pockets. The Greenway scheme would cost only £25,000 and Dartmouth passengers would be taken directly there by steamer. (While the construction was in abeyance there was a coach which met the trains and ran between Churston and Greenway – connecting river boats operated from there to Dartmouth and Totnes). Thus £50,000 would be saved and access to Dittisham, Stoke Gabriel and Blackawton would be improved. It was also canvassed at the time that a railway at high level could be carried over the Dart to join the South Hams Railway. (More correctly this was of course the Kingsbridge & South Devon Railway whose Act had received Royal Assent in 1858). However the Bill was not sanctioned by the House of Lords because of a petition from the owner of Greenway, Mr Harvey, and its failure meant that the original plan of the line to Kingswear could go ahead.

The line to Churston was eventually ready for opening on 14 March 1861:

The Directors' train was met at Brixham Road [as it was called until 1868] by a concourse of spectators numbering upwards of 2,000. The Brixham Volunteer Artillery Corps were lined up while their band played the National Anthem.

In Brixham the day was celebrated with a general holiday; business was at a standstill and so the townspeople flocked to the open fields beside the station, which was bedecked with flags, many clearly being from the signal lockers of the local fishing-smacks. There were booths and stalls of all sorts for the entertainment of the 'aborigines of Brixham, distinguished from the rest by their Guernsey frocks and sou'westers, who drank success to the railway in their own traditional manner'. After the opening there was a rush for the few vehicles in the station yard; those unable to get a seat had to walk back to the town. As the newspaper had warned: 'The station is 2 miles from Brixham, rather an inconvenient distance in unfavourable weather'. There was the inevitable dinner which took place at the London Inn. Paignton had celebrated with its Pudding, so it was only appropriate that Brixham should celebrate with the product which had made her famous – so a fish dinner was arranged at 13s.6d a head. Unfortunately, for days before the opening, easterly gales had prevented the fishing fleet from going to sea but fortunately it was remembered that a splendid turbot had been dispatched to Bristol earlier. The telegraph was put to work and it was confirmed that it remained unsold. Packed in ice it had stayed fresh and was returned by mail train, arriving just in time to save Brixham's reputation.[7]

At the next Company meeting a discussion took place as to the expediency of planting the land in the vicinity of the railway at Paignton with rushes, but it was resolved that no action be taken after one shareholder had stated that their presence were 'calculated to give visitors passing through the town an impression that the place was damp'.

Under resident engineer H.W.Farley, the contractors Blenkinson and Atkinson pushed ahead by tunnelling under the high ground between Galmpton and the river, crossed the two creeks at Noss to reach Hoodown. After passing through cuttings there was a tunnel

(492 feet long) through trap rock and dry slate, where the builders had trouble with water. On leaving the line was carried over the Greenway viaduct (500 feet long, 100 feet high) with ten arches and substantially built of stone and over two wooden viaducts at Longwood and Noss Creeks. Where the navvies were quartered is something of a mystery, as the time of construction coincided with the taking of the 1861 Census. It appears likely that the enumerators would have listed the 'railway labourers' in large numbers; however there are only a few recorded as 'lodgers' at private houses in Brixham and Churston. Perhaps there was a lull in the building work so those engaged at a 'no work, no pay' time had moved on, to return when operations resumed.

The End of the Line – Trains reach Kingswear.
The first train arrived at Kingswear drawn by the engine *Lion*. The complete 'Torquay to Dartmouth' line was opened for passenger traffic on 16 August 1864.[8] Goods had to await the completion of the quays. These took some time to construct, the cost being met jointly by the Company and the Dartmouth Harbour Commissioners. A goods shed was also built and a travelling steam crane bought to ease the transfer of goods between railway and vessels. For the first four weeks after the opening Dartmouth passengers were taken across by the paddle-tug *Pilot* until the iron paddler *Newcomin* entered service. The whole undertaking had cost some £262,000 instead of the £90,000 envisaged when the Company was set up. It was worked by the South Devon on behalf of the Dartmouth & Torbay according to the 1858 Agreement. Two years later the former turned the running over to the latter in perpetuity and henceforward had only a financial existence.

Soon afterwards a publicity notice appeared: 'The South Devon means to destroy grumbling by anticipating everybody's wishes and prevent competition by leaving no ground for discontent for a rival to plant his foot upon'. It went on to announce the 'Dart Trip' – train to Totnes, the River boat to Dartmouth, then back home by rail via Torquay. This almost incomprehensible introduction concluded thus: 'This arrangement will any weekday ensure a trip on the English Rhine'. With short interruptions because of Wars the 'Dart Trip' continued to please for over a century.

Tapestry in black and white: Kingswear in the snow, 1907

Two years later the Royal Dart Hotel opened with an eye on the passengers expected to join the out-going Mail steamers – the traffic failed to arrive but the Hotel, looking little different after over 120 years, remains as an example of Victorian enterprise.[9]

Dartmouth station was built complete with ticket-office, waiting and cloak rooms just like any other railway station but the trains of course were across the Dart at Kingswear. For well over a century it remained

Kingswear Station, 1865/6.

Wooden viaducts near Kingswear, about 1880
Note Britannia and Hindustan in background

Dartmouth Station, 1890s
(Note Kingsbridge Coach, with 'third horse' for hills to Torcross)

the 'only railway station without trains'. In earlier days the *Dolphin* which carried passengers over the water was shown in the Railway Timetable. In deference to local church-people, however, it ran on weekdays only; travellers on Sundays had to resort to private charters.

It is impossible to please everybody and only four days after the opening of the line to Kingswear a meeting was held in Torquay's largest hotel which was attended by the gentry and business people for miles around: it was called to express 'dissatisfaction with the present Company' (the South Devon) and called for a second line from Exeter through South Devon into Torbay. This turned out to be an oblique way of drumming up support for the proposed **Teign Valley Railway Company**, which was having great difficulty at Parliamentary level with its Bill because the South Devon saw it, not surprisingly, as a potential rival. The Teign Valley was to be a *standard gauge* railway and when finally built 18 years later it only ran from Chudleigh Road (later Heathfield) to Ashton, a small isolated village half-way up the Teign

Valley. This branch and the other local ones are dealt with more fully in Chapter 6 below.

The attraction of a railway through the South Hams first appears in a prospectus which appeared in November 1859, indicating the intention of the **Plymouth and South Hams Railway Company** to promote a Bill for a line '... from Plympton St Mary [through] Loddiswell, Torcross, Slapton, Dittisham and terminating at the Floating Bridge Tavern, Dartmouth'. This failed to materialise but the seeds had been sown! Five years later the arrival of the railway at Kingswear across the River encouraged a Dartmouth group to call a public meeting to solicit support for a 'South Hams Railway'. It was to be a so-called 'loop line' from Newton to Dartmouth, Kingsbridge and through to Plymouth. It was proposed to cross the Dart by a bridge at Maypool and from thence through Lower Norton Vale and past Slapton Sands. It was pointed out that 'the tradesmen of Dartmouth are just beginning to reap the first benefits of a railway to the town, and it is now their duty and their interest to extend the benefit and enable the inhabitants of the neighbourhood ... to participate in its advantages'. The idea failed to gain support: a more eccentric proposal to construct a 2ft 6in gauge line from Kingsbridge to the sea at Slapton did not either.

This was not the end of the South Hams story. In the late 1890s plans were deposited for the **Devon, South Hams Light Railway Company** which envisaged a railway, in four sections, from Totnes down the west bank of the Dart through Dittisham to Dartmouth, then through Stoke Fleming and Slapton to Kingsbridge and Yealmpton. A branch line to Salcombe was also proposed.[10] Like so many other fanciful schemes the finance was not forthcoming and the land between the Dart and the Salcombe Estuary has remained relatively unspoilt.

V TRAVELLING IN THE 1850s, 60s and 70s

Complaining letter-writers to newspapers are as old as the Press. 'Disgusted of Tunbridge Wells' is no new phenomenon. Not long after the railway opened to Torquay a correspondent in the *Torquay Directory* complained:

> The Station is far too small and totally inadequate for the purpose required. Goods which arrive in the trucks at 7.30 am are still there at noon, from want of room on the platform to unload them. Goods for forwarding are held for a day and a night before they can be sent from the inability of the porters to find room for loading. When stage-wagons ran, parties could generally depend of receiving their goods at a fixed time but the management is a disgrace to the Company.

In October 1864 another letter appeared signed 'Telegraph Wires' which opened with the statement: 'At a public meeting an assertion was made by *Sir* Lawrence Palk [who was clearly still unfriendly towards the Dartmouth and Torbay] that no train arrived at Torquay Station within ten minutes of the time appointed'. This had brought an emphatic and positive denial from the Company. The anonymous writer however, had conducted a survey of all the principal arrivals in September, nearly 140 in all, and had found that only *five* had arrived on time; the remainder varying from one to 40 minutes late, with one over an hour and five minutes behind time! *Sir* Lawrence's complaint was justified.

Vandalism is not a twentieth century disease either. In May 1856 'a large cable used for hauling carriages on to the main line was thrown across the rails at Kingskerswell'. A train passed right over it without coming off the rails. It also proves that some years after the demise of the atmospheric, man or horse-power was still being used for marshalling purposes!

The novelty of travelling by rail brought problems to some passengers as this story which appeared in the *Torquay Directory* in February 1853 tells:

> At St Thomas Station a gentleman in a first class carriage, in his anxiety to alight, did not wait until the train had duly arrived at the platform, but opened the door of his carriage, and walked out, – not upon the plaform – but over the parapet of the viaduct into a potatoe [sic] garden below ... a fall of upwards of twenty-one feet. Some consternation was felt by the porters; but upon looking over the parapet; they were astounded to see the gentleman quietly looking for his spectacles.

The first 'named train' to serve Torquay was the *Flying Dutchman* in 1862. This originally started running in 1849 and was named after the Derby and St Leger winner of that year. After two years its destination was changed to Plymouth to where it ran for many years. Crack stage-coaches traditionally had names like *Quicksilver*, *Vivid* and *Nautilus*; the railways when they came into existence continued the practice.

Travellers soon found improvements being made for their comfort at least on stations. In August 1860 private enterprise was allowed to open a refreshment room at Torquay Station. Mr Cash of the Queens Hotel paid a rent of £50 a year to the Dartmouth & Torbay. The first railway stations were very small and bleak affairs; another modest step was taken a year later when a small waiting room was built on the up-platform there.

By Train to Bathe at Dawlish

One of the things which brought the watering places into existence was the 'use of sea-water in the treatment of the glands'. Wealthy invalids 'took the waters' but the coming of the railway to South Devon enabled 'other classes to take a dip in the briny' too. A guidebook of about 1860 says of Dawlish, in language worthy of Gerald Hoffnung:

Looking down on Dawlish Station, 1880s

Looking towards Teignmouth, 1880s

The sea-bathing here from the slight inclination of the beach and the firmness of the sands, is of the best description and the climate is said to be milder than of any other Devon watering places, especially in the winter when the village is thronged with respectable visitors. The bathing machines are correspondingly numerous. The bathing place for gentlemen is at Coryton Cove, where abundance of improved accommodation is offered by two distinct companies at the low charge of 5d including towel and drawers. A bathing train leaves St Thomas Station at 7 am during the summer. The return ticket is only 6d. One hour is allowed for bathing, passengers returning by the next up train.

The railway was used by the nobility of Europe. The coming of a Russian Grand Duke in September 1860 was an extraordinary event, reported in full by the *Torquay Directory*: 'The inhabitants of Torquay should feel proud their town has become the favourite resort of the Russian Imperial family'. The Grand Duke Michel and a 'numerous suite' arrived by a special train direct from Dover. The train was met by a large guard of honour provided by the Volunteer Riflemen, who presented arms as he alighted from his carriage. Their Band rather inappropriately played *God Save the Queen*. When he left a month later 'he took his seat in one of the royal carriages which had been sent expressly for his accommodation. After expressing his entire satisfaction with all the arrangments made by the South Devon Railway ... he presented Mr J.P.Morgan, District Superintendent, with a valuable garnet ring, set in diamonds, and Mr Chapman, Superintendent at Torquay, with a handsome diamond breast pin'. Just one example of the opulence of the rulers of Imperial Russia.

When Queen Sophia of Holland came to Torquay to stay ten years later she and her suite arrived by train; she too was given a 'red-carpet' welcome before being whisked off to the Imperial Hotel in a carriage loaned by Angela (later Baroness) Burdett Coutts. The Baroness was just one of the eminent people who had moved into the district; on another occasion she entertained Louis Napoleon and his family. They too of course travelled down by broad-gauge express on their way to the newly-built Imperial Hotel.

All South Devon engines were fitted with two brake (also 'break' in some newspapers) whistles; one with a deep tone, the other with a high-pitched one.[1] The deep-tone indicated the driver wished the brakes on the carriages to be applied and it thus became known as the 'brake whistle' – the first mention of it locally appears in the report of the Boxing Day 1851 incident. The other was used for all other purposes including the signal to 'release the brakes'; fortunately there does not seem to have been confusion in these calls on the South Devon. Before the arrival of more sophisticated systems brakes were only provided on carriages which carried guards, hence the problems which arose when trains had to be stopped in an emergency.

It must have been the primitive nature of the signals and points which worried the South Devon directors to the greatest extent. Of the mishaps which occurred it was the one which took place at Torquay

Kingskerswell Station, about 1854

Station in April 1868 which received the most publicity and if the reports are read fully show how many more worse accidents could have happened. A train of excursionists arrived at Torquay and the train's engine had to be taken back to Torre to be reversed: on its return it was coupled to the carriages which were standing on the middle line between the up and down tracks. The pointsman called Michelmore however failed to reset the points after its return but put the signal to 'clear' when a luggage train from Newton was sent down. This crashed into the stationary train killing one of the drivers and injuring two other train-crew. Michelmore ran off but gave himself up to the Police two days later. On the instructions of the Coroner he was charged with manslaughter. It was however the Report of Colonel Yolland, the Inspector of Railways which shows how lax the safety arrangements then were. He recorded:

> When this portion was opened in 1859 the inter-locking of points and signals had only just been introduced, was by no means general, and was not employed anywhere on the broad-gauge. The South Devon Railway should without delay instruct their engineer to connect the working of points and signals at all their stations, so that similar collisions may not occur again.

Saxby first put signals and point levels into a single long frame with a form of inter-locking between them but as will be seen shortly it took a long time to be achieved. One other paragraph deserves to be chronicled: 'I am informed that there are difficulties in carrying out my suggestions as regards the Torquay and some other stations, inasmuch the company mostly use the eastern or down line for both up and down traffic because there are so many invalids arriving at and leaving the place and would complain at having to cross the opposite platform, and because there is frequently a large amount of heavy baggage to be carried across'. The needs of the customer always came first in those days.

The first of a batch of five accidents took place at Hollacombe near the Gasworks; there were no injuries and it does show how primitive the signalling arrangements were then. The accident is almost unique,

– a photograph taken soon after it happened on 26 September 1866 shows the methods used by the salvage crews at the time. It also shows how basic were the third class carriages. The workmen were laying a switch, as points to a siding were then called; when the train came up from Paignton they had not finished doing it. Neither signal nor flagman was considered necessary.

A Near Disaster at Kingswear.
This was followed by one at Kingswear in May 1870:

> An act of negligence which although providentially not attended with any serious results, was one that only narrowly escaped causing a frightful sacrifice of human life. The 1.15 pm train instead of continuing along the main line, dashed into a siding, smashing a gate closed across the entrance. The driver of the engine, on seeing the danger at once reversed and sounded the break whistle. The two guards had previously discovered the train had gone into the siding and had put on their breaks but before it could be stopped the engine came to a turntable, the rails of which were standing in a contrary direction to those on which the train was coming which had the effect of throwing the engine off and assisted in bringing the train to a standstill, as well as preventing an awful calamity, as the rails only extend about 30 ft further and overhang the harbour into which the train must have fallen if it had not been stopped.[2]

A further accident which happened five years later nearby really was accidental: 'The train which left Newton at 11.36 am narrowly missed falling into the River Dart. Coming out of Maypool tunnel the driver noticed both front wheels of the engine were off the line. He immediately applied his breaks but as the train was travelling at 30 mph down the steep incline it went another mile before it could be pulled up. It stopped just where the bank is between 70 and 100 feet above the river'.

Scenario for a silent movie – the runaway train.
Later in the year an event which started at Torquay Station, might have been the basic script of an early silent screen epic:

> The first up train of the day reached Torquay at 7.35 am and waited there for the goods train from Torre to pass, the line on this branch being single. The goods train, heavily laden, came on at a great speed and the men in charge of it were unable to pull it up. It ran past the danger signal and then a collision with the passenger train was imminent. The drivers of both locomotives reversed their engines; the driver and fireman of the passenger train leapt off. Many of the passengers, in great alarm, struggled frantically to get off and in the confusion several were flung along the platform; some narrowly escaped rolling off the platform on to the rails. One train then collided with the other and the passenger train , having full steam on, sped back towards Paignton at a tremendous rate and has been described as flying through Paignton station. The station-master [at Torquay] attempted to get on her but his assisting people out of the way prevented him ... he then directed that the engine of the goods train be detached and he set off in pursuit. [After the train had passed through Goodrington] ... two men whose names were Edward Purcell and Robert Harley, two platelayers, who were employed repairing the line and happened to be travelling on the train, got out and proceeding from carriage to carriage succeeded in getting to the engine and shutting off steam, bringing it to a standstill on the viaduct near Churston after it had travelled a distance of quite 4 miles. Hadn't the train been providentially brought up it would have passed through Brixham Road, and then acquiring greater velocity going down the incline, must have gone down the embankment into the River Dart.[3]

The driver and fireman of the passenger train were dismissed. Purcell and Harley were rewarded by public subscription and by the directors of the Company.

Yet another accident was modest by comparison: 'The driver of a goods train in a siding at Newton Abbot not noticing the signal which protects the siding was against him ... ran over the points on to the down line. Realising what he had done he at once reversed back but could not reach safety in time. The driver of the passenger engine *Hawk*, nearly new, saw the danger and sounded his break whistle. Although all the breaks were applied the train could not be pulled up ... There were between three and four hundred people on the train; many were shaken but none seriously injured but several ladies were however removed in a fainting state'. That accident took place on New Year's Day 1876 and the official histories note: 'This year the vacuum brake was tried out experimentally but it was several years later that it became standard equipment'.

A long-serving railwayman, Charles Brewer, recalled many years later the situation on the GWR when he started in 1881. Each train consisted of three six-wheeled coaches and an engine. If an extra coach was attached a man was detailed to ride in the extra van, which was usually allocated to boxes of fish. The instruction to him was that, if the van break away, he was to apply the brake which was above the

Accident at Hollacombe, Preston, Paignton, 1865
(Note jacks, etc. being used to engine from toppling over)

wheels. 'Parliamentary trains' were still running a 1d a mile. He also said that railway staffs were then working 14 hours a day with no Sundays off.

Over the years Newton Abbot was, until recently, the centre of the railway system in South Devon there. However A.J.Rhodes wrote disparagingly of its first station as being 'nothing more than tumble-down sheds'.[4] Newton (it was not Newton Abbot until 1877) was subsequently rebuilt between 1859 and 1861 as a two-sided junction station.[5] A decade later it was being ridiculed:

> Newton Station is an extremely breezy place, being in architectural composition in the form of a tube, which acts as a sucker to the cold winds, consequently one has here the opportunity of enjoying an immense amount of fresh air, and all the benefits of a day out without going any further.[6]

There were problems with the GWR over the supply and mainte-nance of locomotives, which resulted in a contract being made with Charles Geach of Birmingham for their supply for ten years from 1851.[7] Daniel Gooch's younger brother William, was in charge of the contract and also of the South Devon's loco works at Newton 'for although it had only about one dozen engines to work the whole line, it was found necessary to have repairing shops of some kind'. Subse-quently in 1859, when the Cornwall Railway was being opened to Truro, it was proposed that facilities for servicing and repairing all locomotives of the Company, which was to work it as well, should be located at Newton Abbot. As a result the sheds were enlarged considerably. The incoming work-force quickly had problems; in June 1861 it was reported: 'The works ... are becoming of such magnitude and employing such a number of skilled workmen who find a difficulty in finding houses to reside in. To meet this want the South Devon Railway have determined to erect 150 houses near their works for their employees'.

Newton Abbot later owed a great debt to the Great Western because after it assumed control in 1876 it 'provided one of the best benefits that could have fallen on Newton'.[8] The Company greatly extended the locomotive and carriage works; the locomotive capacity was increased from four to 40 and the workers went up to nearly 600. A bank and coal stage was built, the workshops improved and a new set of carriage shops erected at the west end. Offices were built for the superintendent; there was a smith's shop with ten or a dozen forges together with carpenters', painters' and trimmers' shops adjacent. By the 1930s the work-force was one thousand. In 1960 the repair works closed and now nothing remains of an industry which played such a vital part in the economy of South Devon. The large marshalling yard at Hackney, built in 1911, was at one time one of the largest in the west; today it too is derelict and ready for development as an industrial estate.

Newton Abbot Station, 1900s

VI OTHER SOUTH DEVON BRANCH LINES

The Brixham Line and the Torbay and Brixham Railway Company.
Richard Wolston first conceived the vision of a railway to Brixham as
early as 1845 but it is said that the 'battle of the gauges' deterred him.
It was therefore not until August 1861, shortly after a survey by Mr
Julian, an architect, that his proposition was put to a public meeting at
the Subscription Rooms for a railway 'main line to Furzeham Common, high above the town, so there would be no personal jealousy as to
who should benefit most'. He told the meeting, which was widely
reported in Devon newspapers, that he had researched in the Books of
H. M. Customs at Dartmouth and these showed how prosperous the
town was. Belonging to Brixham owners were 110 vessels valued at
£160,000 trading to all parts of the world, and 110 fishing boats worth
£60-70,000. It was probably from Julian's figures that he estimated the
cost of the venture would be £13,000, which he thought was a great
deal for just 7,000 local residents to raise. He therefore was not going
to ask for £600, £700 nor £1,000 from each subscriber – just £10. He
considered the line would be profitable; 'had not the Dartmouth and
Torbay Railway when the line only extended to Paignton carried
104,577 passengers in the 6 months to December 1860, realising them
nearly £1,000'.

The residents were unconvinced and matters moved but slowly as
they were not ready to contribute even this small amount in any
numbers (some say that he only asked £2 from each). When the notice
of the incorporation of the **Torbay and Brixham Railway Company**
appeared, it included details of the proposed line 'from the Parish of
Churston Ferrers ... by a Junction with the Siding of the Dartmouth &

73

Torbay Railway ... and terminating at a point at the southern end of Furzeham Common'. From there a tramway was to continue a further 21 chains 'wholly situated in the Parish of Brixham' to the north-eastern corner of the Common (this part was never proceded with and it has been suggested recently[1] that this did not materialise because the output from Wolston's iron mine there was already declining.

The Bill went before Parliament on Wolston's personal application early in 1864 and it received Royal Assent in December. While this was before the House of Lords Committee a special meeting of the Dartmouth and Torbay was called to approve certain clauses. One concerned the gauge (it was broad of course); another confirmed that the two companies should work together, each having access to the other's lines, etc. These were duly agreed, providing, as one shareholder put it, there was 'nothing requiring the Dartmouth and Torbay to give pecuniary assistance to the Torbay and Brixham Railway'. When the amount eventually subscribed by the public was insufficient, Wolston, on his own initiative, took 1770 of the 1800 shares; the remaining 30 being held by two relatives and a friend. He was something of a character, a man of many parts; he was described in the Company documents as being a solicitor but he also owned iron mines, marketed *Wolston's Torbay Iron Paint*, made sewerage pipes and ironstone pottery.

In spite of last-minute problems the opening took place on 1 January 1868 though passenger trains did not run until the end of February.[2] The original contractor had defaulted so Wolston took over the task and completed the project at his own expense. The line was only two and half miles long and ran through picturesque and undulating country. There were seven bridges, five of stone and two of wood, built by Mr Lyte of Brixham: the cuttings were all cut through hard lime-rock by Mr William George. Brixham Station was constructed by Mr Maddock, who also did all the carpentry work. In our age of 'sub-contractors', it is interesting to see this early example so many years ago. Water to supply the engines was taken from the Mill Leat and from the stream which then ran down behind Bolton Street (although now culverted it still does), being raised the 135 feet by a water-wheel. Wolston bought the necessary land in the town centre near the present Town Hall and this subsequently became the property of the Great Western Railway.[3] A new road was carved out of the hillside from Quay to Station; the trains have long-since gone but that steep and tortuous climb to the Green remains to torment motorists – but the view of Torbay from the top is magnificent. The little railway offered not only a fine view to the east as far as the Dorset coast, but also to the west where the Dartmoor hills formed a massive back-drop.

On Christmas Eve 1867 the test train headed by *Ajax*, one of the heaviest South Devon engines weighing 38 tons, went along the route. The standard of workmanship 'was found to answer every expectation'. The novelty of the event 'attracted a large crowd of inhabitants, particularly sturdy fishermen of the port, who cheered as only sailors can cheer and drank Mr Wolston's health with their usual blunt and hearty good cheer, accompanied with the usual three, and three times over, after which they were treated to a ride as far as Brixham Road'. On the opening day a special train left Newton Abbot at noon; it arrived at Brixham Road half an hour later drawn by the South Devon's engine *Lance*, decorated with flags and evergreens on the last two miles of its inaugural journey. Waiting at Brixham was a large crowd and three bands: the Torquay Subscription, the Torquay Fife and Drum and the Brixham Artillery. For the day-to-day running of the Branch Wolston bought secondhand the small engine *Queen*, built by Wilson of Leeds and used during the construction of Portland breakwater. The rest of the rolling stock was hired from the South Devon, which managed, staffed and worked it.

In those early years the Railway made a considerable contribution to Brixham's prosperity. 800 tons of fish were carried in the first year; by 1877 the weight had risen to 2,000 and a decade later to 2,600. In the six months to December 1868 passenger returns showed that 1,044 had travelled First Class; 12,902 Second and 21,137 Third. The half-yearly Directors' Meeting was also told that from May 1869 travellers from Brixham could book to any destination; previously they had to take fresh tickets at Churston.

The periodic accounts rendered by the South Devon showed it was making considerable losses on its operations and Wolston was forced to mortgage *Queen* as security. He also had to dispose of half the capital of

Torbay & Brixham's engine Queen
(From Brixham Museum's picture collection)

the Company to a Henry Ellis, and a Charles Ashford was appointed Secretary.[4] Either because of this or because of suggestions by Wolston's friends, an experienced accountant was brought in to examine the figures. He found that by an ingenious scheme income was being grossly under-estimated by the South Devon in their favour. After unsuccessful negotiations the case was referred to the Railway Commission. One of the devices used by the South Devon to delay the resolution of the affair was to insist that the required figures were 'not available'. *Sir* Frederick Peel, when delivering the Commission's judgement said that 'there should be no difficulty in finding out the sum due to the Brixham Company and that it should be paid in one calendar month'. Revised figures were eventually produced and these now included revised and exorbitant charges for the use of the station at Churston. A further appeal was made to the Railway Commission who once more found in favour of the Torbay & Brixham, which was then awarded £2,000 damages and well as its claim in full. By the time this case had been resolved the Great Western Railway had absorbed the South Devon Railway.

However the little Brixham Company determined to continue on its own. Under the original Act the Company was only authorised to raise capital of £18,000 and to borrow on mortgage a further £6,000. Not surprisingly these had been insufficient to meet both costs and interest payments and the latter had been, and were still accumulating, so it had to go to the expense of obtaining a further Act to stabilise its finances. The Act (38 Vict. c.32) was passed in 1875 and included a clause which authorised conversion to the 'narrow or mixed gauge' if both the South Devon and Dartmouth and Torbay went ahead. It seems that the Torbay and Brixham realised the broad gauge was doomed long before its larger neighbour!

The Great Western sold the Company an ex-SDR engine called *Raven* and hired all the carriages and goods wagons it needed. The Torbay & Brixham became responsible for all staffing and worked the enterprise itself; in 1878 we find Andrew Wood with the grandiose title

Brixham 'Whippet' waits at Churston, c.1910

Stationmaster at Brixham and Superintendent of the Line. In 1883 it too sold out to the GWR for £12,000.

Rail travel between Churston and Brixham prospered for many years; in 1895 there were ten trains each way on weekdays. At some stage the diminutive train became known as the *Brixham Whippet* and as such is remembered with affection by many local people who, as children, made the term-time journey on it twice a day to and from school in Torquay. As late as 1959 the branch was well-used; there were 12 trains a day during the week and 17 on Saturdays. There was only one goods train, though fish vans were attached to the up passenger train in the evening at Churston by a curious little ritual, which took the whole Brixham auto-train on to the main line to do the shunting. After the demise of steam a three-coach diesel unit was used during the summer but a single rail-car sufficed in the winter. This one's last journey was in the early evening while the bus company ran into the town centres until late at night – the end was therefore inevitable. The Brixham Branch closed down in 1963 as it was then costing £10,000 a year to run.

The Moretonhampstead Line

A preliminary public meeting was held at the Globe Hotel in Newton Abbot in August 1858 when the desirability of a line to Moretonhampstead was discussed but the real impetus came in late 1860 when the Devon Central Railway Bill was promoted. This went before Parliament in the 1861 Session and provided for the building of lines from Exeter north-west to Moretonhampstead, Chagford, Okehampton & Lydford and west to Chudleigh and Newton. Both were rejected but it inspired the South Devon to promote its broad-gauge **Moretonhampstead & South Devon Railway Company** which was incorporated in 1862 (Its Act, 25/26 Vict.c.128, received Royal Assent the same year).[5] For a short distance it followed the line of James Templer's Haytor Granite Railway which had opened in 1820 and used horse-power only. It is not part of this story and has been dealt with in detail elsewhere.[6]

The opening four years later on 4 July 1866 'was not attended by any sort of demonstration on the route'. Being market day in Newton 'the traffic from Moreton and Bovey was great ... the whole of the carriages

Moretonhampstead Station, about 1890
(Note broad gauge carriage at platform)

of the first train, the 9.50 am were full and at every station large wondering crowds were gathered to witness the arrival of the train'. An agent of Brassey and Ogilvie (the builders) accompanied the engine-men on every journey that day so that they could familiarize them-selves with the curves and gradients. Eager to prove the safety of the new addition to the transport scene, a newsman wrote in the *Torquay Directory*:

> Two of the heaviest goods engines that were at hand, with carriages coupled together, were placed at the disposal of Colonel Yolland, Government Inspector of Railways for testing the line. The whole of the bridges were severely tested; the train was drawn across them slowly then at high speed and ultimately brought to a standstill on them. All were found to be soundly built.

GWR bus at Moretonhampstead, late 1900s

The work had been carried out during an exceptionally bad winter (January 1866 had seen the Great Hurricane sweep South Devon), and the almost continuous rain had held up progress but according to the Engineer 'had a beneficial effect of consolidating the embankments'.

It is often through the reports of Company meetings that the prosperity or otherwise of these early railways could be judged; in August 1870 it was noted that there had been 43,400 passengers in the previous six months, compared with 41,300 in the same period of 1869. This had produced an increase in revenue of £85.17s.5d – hardly a bonanza for the shareholders. However there was some optimism about future profits as 'hostile clauses in the Bill introduced by the Teign Valley Railway had been withdrawn'. The Teign Valley saga is told briefly below.

Chagford, an ancient stannary and market town, was in the mid-nineteenth century 'on account of the bracing salubrity of its air ... much visited by seekers after health'. Moretonhampstead too had a similar reputation (which is no doubt why in 1929 the GWR bought and converted the magnificient Manor House Hotel, complete with 18-hole golf course, there). After the arrival of the motor bus the

L&SWR buses at Chagford, late 1900s

Company in 1906 introduced its Moretonhampstead to Chagford service, replacing a long-established horse-bus. An early photograph shows that this had a Cornish registration (*AF 139*), as did some of those operating in Torbay about the same time. In 1904 the London & South Western Railway started a rival service to the horse-bus from Queen Street station in Exeter connecting with certain expresses using Clarkson steam buses. They later ran from Yeoford Junction and had a reputation for being unreliable. A contemporary guidebook said of the rival services:

> The distance is about 15 miles, the route being via Crockernwell and Whiddon Down. Passengers by the Great Western Railway can go to Newton Abbot and then change on to the Moreton Hampstead branch, travelling 4½ miles farther by motor-bus, but this is a circuitous route not particularly to be recommended. At the same time the service is more frequent.[7]

As one of the pre-Beeching closures the last passenger trains ran in March 1959. The *Western Morning News* summed it all up thus:

> Wise men looked ahead to the future and saw the railways as means of new prosperity ... Cottages and farmhouses began taking in summer visitors ... Regular agricultural workers got 10/6d a week plus privileges and cider; the railway pointed to regular work in towns at better pay. Between 1862 and 1866 farmers complained of labour shortages, men preferring to work as navvies in the construction of the line.

Some have said that the line should never have been built – its viability must have been in doubt from the start though it did enjoy some popularity in the 1930s. Memories however still remain of the 'Moor train' which left the Torbay towns soon after ten in the morning and took passengers on to the Branch without changing. It called at Teigngrace, Heathfield, Brimley Halt, Bovey Tracey, and Lustleigh on its leisurely way to the terminus at Moreton. The section above Bovey Tracey closed for freight in 1964, the rails being taken up in 1971.[8] The track as far as Heathfield was retained and used for china-clay trains. The future of this line now (1987) seems secure. In December 1986 British Rail's Railfreight committed £4 million to secure 124 new air-braked wagons to replace the existing 30 year-old trucks. Some 30,000 tons of ball-clay are moved annually. It is so named as in former days this product from the Bovey basin was cut into blocks called *balls* for easy lifting.

The Totnes, Ashburton & Buckfastleigh Line.

As outlined in Chapter 1 the coming of 'railway mania' brought unfulfilled plans by several companies to build railways around the southern edge of Dartmoor, that is through Buckfastleigh, Ashburton and Chudleigh, rather than further south and east as eventually happened. After the last attempt in the late 1840s the isolation of the first two towns continued for nearly 15 years. During this time the economies of both suffered a serious decline. In this part of South Devon, as in other parts of the country, the arrival of the railway, in this case at Plymouth, caused the disappearance virtually overnight of the stage-coaches which had provided a lucrative 'passing trade' for well over a century. The local mining or woollen industries had become isolated from their markets too.

Public concern prompted the calling of a meeting in September 1861 to consider the desirability of building a railway from Buckfastleigh to Totnes, at which three different routes were proposed; one necessitated excavating a tunnel near Huxham's Cross. The usual optimistic estimate of cost was made – £600 per mile, exclusive of land. All the landowners involved were said to be in favour but it took two years, until November 1863, for the plans for two railways to be submitted to Devon Quarter Sessions: one for a line from Totnes to Buckfastleigh; the other for a short one from the main line to Totnes Quay. The Buckfastleigh, Totnes and South Devon Railway Act became law on 25 June 1864. A little under twelve months later a second Act was obtained authorising an extension from Buckfastleigh to Ashburton.[9]

A meeting at the Seymour Hotel in Totnes in October 1870 was told that the negotiations with the Ecclesiastical Commissioners were complete and that the contractor was starting work on a section which had been in dispute: meanwhile Buckfastleigh station was built;

Ashburton's was started, as were two bridges over the Dart. However it was 18 months before the line actually opened in May 1872. It took some time longer to get traffic moving to Totnes Quay but it too finally opened in November 1873. It was worked only by horses until August 1874 at which time locomotives were allowed to within 20 yards of the level crossing at the Plains. Horses continued to work the rest until 1948 when approval was given for the use of tractors. The sight of those magnificent animals at work was a delight to all.

This small rural company was to cause a furore only seven years later. As noted below, Mr Jeffrey Michelmore's announcement that his Company was going to apply for a Bill to link Paignton with Totnes was received in Torquay and elsewhere with delight.

The line to Ashburton was always too small and remote to be profitable. In 1906 steam rail-motors were tried without much success. There was some increase in traffic about 1930 but then it was only moderate. BR was looking at the viability of small branch lines before the Beeching era and this was one of those 'axed', closing on 1 November 1958 – the last train's engine being draped with mourning by the town's 'First Citizen', the Portreeve. The Totnes to Ashburton part of the line (the remainder to Ashburton has been replaced by the A38 dual carriageway) was bought by the **Dart Valley Railway Company**, described at the time as 'the first private enterprise commercial railway, run as a public company, in this decade' with a board of eight businessmen directors. The first trains ran in 1969; the livery adopted was of course the chocolate and cream of the Great Western and the DVR insignia is the only indication today that the clock has not been put back 40 years.

The Teign Valley Line

Now little more than a memory, the Teign Valley line ran through some of the most picturesque country in South Devon and it has been suggested recently by Mr Pomroy that 'it must surely be a modeller's paradise'[10] As yet his hope does not seem to have been realised. The **Teign Valley Railway Company** originated in 1863 and its line was to run from Chudleigh Road (later Heathfield) to Chudleigh and Doddiscombsleigh, though endeavours to provide a 'Line of Railway through

Mid-Devon' (the Mid-Devon and Cornwall Railway) had only finally miscarried three years earlier. As a result of that failure, the desirability of setting up 'a United Company ... for accomplishing the Railway accommodation for Central Devon and Launceston, together with a Branch down the Teign to Newton, and to North Devon' had been put forward. The first-named member of the Provisional Committee was *Sir* L.Palk, Bart. He was of course MP for South Devon, but is better remembered as one of the Palks who 'built Torquay' – his interest in railways, however, is not well known. When the Teign Valley Company was formed he became its Chairman and in a statement to a half-yearly meeting he explained:

> The real object of those who promoted the Company was simply this: – The South Devon had refused all extensions in any direction – they refused extensions in every direction – but upon pressure being applied to them by Earl Devon and myself in 1862, Mr Woolcombe began to prepare block lines.

Block lines were manoeuvres to prevent rivals from obtaining essential legislation: a term which crops up elsewhere in Devon. Mr Woolcombe was Chairman of the South Devon and at the Dartmouth opening he announced to the large gathering that he opposed the Teign Valley proposal totally, because 'first it was not necessary, and secondly it would have taken no small share of the profits of the South Devon Railway'. The costs of fighting this opposition finally put the Teign Valley in Chancery and the powers lapsed, but were subsequently revived. In 1875, after turning to the London and South Western it obtained a new Act authorising a standard gauge line to Crediton. This too was abandoned and the Teign Valley Railway finally opened, but only to Ashton, in October 1882 as a standard gauge line, and worked by the Great Western. The initial terms were: 55% of gross receipts with a minimum of £1,200 *per annum*.

One of the more fanciful proposals was for it to be extended through Newton Abbot to St Marychurch. The report of the opening told the story so far:

Station staff pose at Ashton, early 1900s

It had more vicissitudes since its first inception than any other line. The original scheme under the name of the Devon Central Railway, was projected 21 years ago. The Bill was rejected and gave place to the Mid-Devon Railway, which afterwards developed into the Moretonhampstead branch. For whole periods the scheme was practically abandoned and grass covered the track on which the lines were laid. It became a standing joke 'commencing in a field and ending nowhere'.

It then remained an isolated little line, on its own until after the gauge-change in 1892.

The Exeter, Teign Valley & Chagford Railway Company Act of 1883 authorised the building of a railway from St Thomas station to join up with the Teign Valley line. Although there were many meetings over the next decade nothing was done until 1894 when a new Act received Royal Assent. This drew the comment: 'Though it was talked of as long as can be remembered by that important individual "the oldest inhabitant" the scheme for a direct railway between Exeter and the Teign valley is now assuming definite shape' – on 7 November Lady Northcote cut the first sod. There were huge engineering works, some said to be purely to placate the local land-owners, and so the Exeter Railway did not open until June 1903. The decision to abandon the portion to Chagford was made in 1897, mainly it is believed, for financial reasons. Whilst the building was in progress, plans for a Brent, Ashburton and Heathfield Railway (the Mid Devon Railway) were deposited with the Clerk of the Peace in November 1897; this would have provided a third alternative route from Exeter to Plymouth by building a line in two sections from near Heathfield Station, passing through Bickington and west of both Ashburton and Buckfastleigh (with no junction with the existing line) to join the main Totnes-to-Plymouth at South Brent.[11] This might have made the Teign Valley's operation more economic in the medium term. Its proposed route lay along what is now the line of the A38 dual-carriageway between Drum Bridges and South Brent.

In all, nine Acts were needed to get it started. It never did more than offer a meagre passenger service through a rural backwater, though it was well-used on Wednesdays – Market Day in Newton Abbot. Traffic from the various quarries was extensive from the beginning, and continued until the demise of the line. Childhood memories are of a steam rail-motor providing the service from Exeter – the 'footplate' was hot and cramped and a brief journey aboard was not an enjoyable experience for a very young boy. For 50 years, until nationalisation, it formed an alternative emergency route to the more vulnerable main line – a relative recalls more than once seeing a Cornish express going through Chudleigh Knighton in two parts, drawn by tank engines, after one severe storm hit the coast. The *Torbay Express* is also known to have passed that way in similar circumstances. It was a friendly line – there was one driver who would blow his whistle if he arrived in a station before his intending passengers – and then waited for them to arrive!

The end of this, yet another small branch line, came in June 1958. The *South Devon Journal* made it a formal funeral:

Five hundred passengers followed it to the grave. Ceremonial flowers were placed on tank-engine 5533. And Exeter sang 'Auld Lang Syne' as the last train went down the twilight valley ... Some resented the show of mourning. Cries were several: 'Better fit they bought tickets to keep it alive. Instead of riding to the funeral.'

There was considerable truth in this – throughout 1956 there had only been an average of 16 passengers for each train. Some goods and mineral traffic continued to the south of Christow for a year or two but subsequently the rails were removed from this too. As was done between Ashburton and Buckfastleigh, the A38 trunk road has been constructed over part of the original route.

The Exeter City Basin [12]

The City of Exeter pressed strongly for a line to the basin of the Exeter Canal. Eventually Parliamentary approval was obtained in 1864 by the South Devon for a single track, less than half a mile long, starting from a point near St Thomas station. The Act stipulated that it should be mixed-gauge and that it should be able to be used from St David's station by the standard gauge trucks of the London & South Western Railway. The SDR added a third rail, on the down line only, between the two points, so that the daily 'City Basin train' ran in both directions on the down line – a practice which continued well into Great Western days. Broad and standard gauge wagons were linked together for the journey by a 'match-truck', with couplings for either at each end – an odd sight which shows yet again the problems of two different gauges having to work together. It opened on 17 June 1867. The track still dips away from the main line; the principal user today seems to be a road asphalt company. It no longer goes as far as the water, stopping short of the main road to the Marsh Barton industrial estate.

VII NEW OWNERS AND NEW IDEAS

From 1866 the South Devon Railway had full financial and operational control over the line from Torquay to Kingswear. It was bringing new faces in ever-increasing numbers and local people were able to travel around as never before: the next decade was to be very prosperous for the whole of the district. Guidebooks of the day eulogised the new form of transport; readers of one were invited to take *A trip on the South Devon Railway*. In pride of place the first chapter says: 'Of all the beautiful scenery of which this county contains such endless variety; and which numerous railways in other parts of the kingdom have opened to the view of the Tourist, there is none which can outvie in novelty and picturesque effect that which the present line develops throughout its entire length'.

Some indication of the class of person arriving by train can be gauged from the following civic enactment:

> **Regulations for cabs plying for hire
> at Tor and Torquay Stations.**
>
> To places within one mile 1/-
> Beyond that distance 2/-
>
> The Turnpike tolls are to be paid by the passenger.
> The driver is not entitled to any gratuity.

By this time the old Tollhouse in the middle of the Sea Front at Torquay had been abandoned and a new one built adjacent to the

Station; thus all new arrivals, no sooner settled into their carriages and cabs, had to halt to pay the charge before they could continue into Torquay. This irritation only disappeared when the system was abolished in November 1874.

Paignton benefited from the Railway too. There is an unsubstantiated story that the name was changed from Paington to Paignton because of the coming of the railway: on timetables the abbreviation *Pain.* was not considered good for the growing town's image. There was clearly a doubt in the mind of 'the painter who painted Paington on one board and Paignton on another, at the railway station' in 1866. Recording this a letter-writer to the local newspaper reminded readers that 'he had good warranty for his eccentricity' as many people in the place did not know which was the more correct.

The same early guidebook says of Paignton: 'This little village as it appeared only a few years since, is now, from the increase of buildings, villas. &c; become the abode of a genteel resident population and a place of resort for invalids'. Brixham, on the other hand, was dismissed thus: 'This place has made some progress in a new and better class of buildings, especially in the higher part of the town ... the lower part near the quay still stands in need'.

Dartmouth had prospered too: 'the introduction of the Railway to this town has caused great attractions and improvements to be made ... streets and roads, where formerly two vehicles could not pass each other, have been widened'. The present-day visitor who throngs the narrow, crowded streets of the town must be thankful that they are walking the *improved* thoroughfares. The guidebook's introduction to the charms of Dartmouth still hold good a century later: 'The stranger, accustomed to the straight, monotonous brick-and-mortar rows of a modern street, will be much struck with the projecting fronts, carved brackets, and antique gables of this old but interesting town'. The railway navvies also enriched knowledge of the ancient town; Dartmouth was stormed and taken by Fairfax during the Civil War: 'Some curious remains of these conflicts have recently been brought to light while making the railway, in the shape of cannon balls, some of which were encased in lead and a granite shot was recently disentombed'.

Jack Metherell started work on the railway in 1867. Fifty years later the plight of Third-class passengers was still clear in his memory: 'They were forced to rise very early in the day and catch a train soon after 7 o'clock in the morning. Those [trains] which left at more reasonable hours were for First and Second class passengers only'. This was the subject of national comment and ridicule: 'Let a servant man or woman apply for a ticket they will be told that 3rd class carriages are only for labourers ... For many years people around stations tried to prevent the better classes from travelling third!'[1]

The Gauge War
The battle as to which gauge should serve the West Country started in the very earliest days. The Great Western's first attempt to build a railway (in 1834) failed and in part this failure was due to the efforts of the **London & Southampton Railway Company**, whose Bill was successful. The latter therefore had a year's start and by 1840 the line to Southampton was complete – though the GWR had only reached Reading. By then the Company's name had been changed to the **London & South Western Railway Company**.[2] As noted earlier, in the 1850s Joseph Locke, (the engineer) and his contractor Thomas Brassey (they had worked together on railways in France in the 1830s) gave support to the **Salisbury & Yeovil Railway Company**; the London and South Western then joined in the fray and authorization was obtained by the former to take the railway through to Exeter. Parliament stipulated, however, that the whole project was to be completed by 1861 or the share-holders would have their dividends stopped! The first passenger train entered the station in the centre of the City in July 1860, thus completing what had first been proposed some 15 years earlier.

Having established itself at Central Station the Company soon continued the tracks down the slope to St David's Station which already had the broad gauge lines of the Bristol & Exeter coming in from the north and those of the South Devon from the south. Furthermore they took over traffic operations north of the City towards Barnstaple, after dubious goings-on by the various contenders for the north Devon lines. It also, through its ally the Devon Central Railway, in September 1860 surveyed land right in enemy territory – in the centre of Torquay near Upton Church.

Although not at first sight part of this story, the Chairman of the the South Devon Railway was perhaps complacent when he told a meeting at Plymouth in 1860 that he was quite unperturbed at the possibility of a line through Okehampton, Launceston, and 'down the backbone of Cornwall' – the one daily [four-horse] coach to Tavistock 'did not load well and it was apprehended that a two-horse coach would be substituted; the South Western were unlikely to expend their money upon a barren district'. However, before long, the **Okehampton Railway Company** had been formed to construct a line around the north of Dartmoor from Exeter! After many hiccups and delays this had been built beyond Okehampton, to Tavistock and finally into Devonport and Plymouth, bringing standard gauge South Western trains into the latter by 1876.

Clerical gentlemen are well-known for their interest in railway matters. This is obviously a long-standing one, for among the earliest people to show enthusiasm for railway travel was one Canon Tetley, who graphically described his early journeys on West Country trains. There was, he said, no refreshment room at Torquay but told of a 'quaint sort of booth which had been established in a field nearby where an old couple provided an excellent cup of tea'.

The urge to build Torquay Station in the town centre continued throughout the decade. There was a public meeting in June 1866 when one local worthy, feeling the station at Torre was 'inconveniently distant from the town' demanded a committee be formed to consider and report to yet another meeting. This was immediately negated by another worthy – and so the matter lay dormant for five years, until, in November 1871, a well-attended meeting declared in favour of extending the railway to the harbour. A few days later an even larger gathering passed a resolution to the contrary. This playing off of one against the other resumed in November 1873 when a public meeting convened to demand 'increased railway accommodation' passed a resolution asking the London & South Western to extend its railway from Exeter to Torquay! Previous attempts to minimise competition between the two Companies had taken place in 1867 and in 1871-2 but the **Associated Companies** (that is, the GWR, the South Devon, the

Bristol & Exeter, the Cornwall Railway and the West Cornwall) were at a disadvantage against the single-managed L&SWR and therefore a merger would provide a unified front to its expansionist policies.

The South Devon directors were beginning to have long-term worries too. In 1873 they had promised Torquay Local Board of Health that they would replace 'that unpretentious little structure which has done duty for so many years' – the rebuilding of Torquay Station was now urgent.

A third track was laid to Aller and the Torquay branch became separate again in 1874, but there were still between 12 and 14 miles of the main line between Totnes and Plymouth to be doubled. Similar work was also needed between Kingskerswell and Torquay; the total cost of it all was thought to be between three-quarters and one million pounds. This did not include even more urgent work at Plymouth. Late in 1875 a special Meeting of the directors was told that the Great Western Railway had assets of over 50 million pounds and so the final consent to the hand-over of control was given within the day; the share-holders of the GWR were not so sure and confirmation was only given after a long discussion.

On New Years Day 1876 directors of the GWR visited Torquay and met leading citizens concerning the 'improved railway accommodation' which had been desired for so long. Sir Daniel Gooch represented the GWR; Dr Radclyffe Hall, W.Kitson, Mr Luxmoore and J.T.Harvey, the Town. The meeting was held 'one very cold night in the little shanty which has done duty as a waiting room for so long a period' on the up platform.[3] The first difficulty the GWR encountered in Torbay was a demand for the end of the 'branch line' image. It was urged to abandon that 'dangerous portion from Newton to Totnes that Brunel had unwisely taken across thinly-populated moor, whereas if he had brought round southwards, a rich and teeming country would be opened up ... it was still not too late, Paignton and Totnes could still be linked'. Gooch dismissed it out of hand as it would cost £250,000. The South Hams alternative (a line across the River Dart to Plymouth) was still alive: even while this debate was raging a Kingsbridge man was spending £400 of his own money researching the feasibilty of building a three foot six inch gauge line there.

The merger took effect from 1 February, when the Great Western Railway became masters from Paddington to Penzance; Paddington would now be in control from a single base, just as its rival had long been able to do from Waterloo.[4] By May double tracks to Kingskerswell had been completed and the intention to double the line from Kingskerswell to Torquay was announced. Perhaps the 'runaway train' episode, told earlier, was the trigger for this improvement. Clearly it was Torquay, the fastest growing town in the area, which was providing the cash-flow with its large passenger and goods traffic, and therefore the GWR was prepared to take prompt action to improve the Station. That a new facility might also take the edge off demands for the line to Totnes may have been in the directors' minds too.

By February 1877:

> The army of excavators and other workmen have effected a complete transformation in the neighbourhood of Torquay Station. Scores of trees have been felled, hedges removed, bridges taken down, the railway cutting widened to about four times its original width, [and] broad embankments have been thrown up.

All was ready and the contract for the new station was given to Messrs Vernon & Ewens of Cheltenham. Construction took over a year and in July 1878 the 'up' platform was opened. On 1 September the old Torquay Station closed after the 7.32 pm had left and the first issue of tickets from the new one took place for the 8.26 pm down train. This elegant Victorian building has now been listed as being of architectural importance. The demolition of the 'unpretentious little structure' started the next day. A few days later Saxby's Patent signals came into use at the new station, just ten years after Colonel Yolland had urged their introduction. The improvements included a new booking office in the most frequented part of the town (on Vaughan Parade) which remained in operation for a century; Torquay's visitors were not expected to go to its fringes for tickets. Paignton day-trippers, on the other hand, had to come to Torquay for theirs.

The intention to link Torbay with Totnes continued to occupy the attention of many influential people in the district from time to time.

In October 1878 a report appeared of a Buckfastleigh Railway Company meeting, at which Jeffrey Michelmore had announced the proposal to apply for a Bill to link Paignton with Totnes by rail. A public meeting held at Torquay followed on 6 November heartily supported the scheme. Early in 1880 a second public meeting passed a firm resolution in favour of completing the line between Totnes and Paignton 'in order to place Torquay on the main line'.[5] Within months a Bill had passed through Parliament and itbecame law on 12 August 1880 as the Totnes, Paignton, and Torquay Direct Railway Act (43 & 44 Vict. c.161). This proposed two railways: the first of 4 furlongs, 7½ chains from the GWR line near Totnes Station to Berry Pomeroy, whilst the second would be 6 miles 1 furlong long – from the termination of the first, and ending in the parish of Paignton at a junction with the Torquay and Dartmouth line. The directors included Mr Michelmore, Arthur Champernowne [of Dartington] and others, none of whom appear to have been connected with the Great Western. The capital required was estimated to be £90,000 and there was legal provision for mortgages of up to £30,000. Local critics dismissed the line, as it 'started in a field and ended in a ditch'. There was a short Act (47 & 48 Vict. c.55) to follow four years later, entitled 'An Act for the Abandonment of the Totnes, Paignton and Torquay Direct Railway'. Although strenuous efforts had been made over a three year period, particularly in the Torbay towns, the general lack of support had killed it.

Opposition to the broad gauge was hardening too; in 1882 the Torquay Narrow Gauge and Improvement Society was founded. The activities which went on in the Transfer Shed at Exeter (where many goods had to be changed from 'standard' to 'broad gauge' trucks) made operations uneconomic. It was noted that goods shipped from the Midlands to the London Docks and then brought by sea cost 20/- a ton; brought by the GWR it cost 40/-! The situation continued to have a high profile, because in November a deputation of local influential personages met the Torquay Local Board of Health concerning the conversion of the gauge 'from broad to narrow'. The deputation agreed to meet the GWR and took with them a petition 30ft long which among other things stated: 'Few families with invalids, unless they are compelled by the advice of their medical adviser, care to come to Torquay and run the risk of changing and being placed in different carriages [at Exeter]. London traffic goes to Bournemouth "the Hampshire Torquay"'. Local papers continued to press the case: 'There is now war to the knife between the Great Western and the London and South Western, and there is nothing to prevent the latter in conjunction with the Midland Railway pushing into Devon and constructing a line from Exeter to Torquay and possibly through the South Hams to Plymouth'.

As early as 1872 the South Western had allowed Third Class passengers on its West Country expresses; five years later it abandoned 'express fares' (higher charges on fast trains) and the Great Western was forced to do likewise but *only to the stations where it was in competition*. Passengers became more and dissatisfied as the years went by; 1882 was a very difficult one for the GWR. In the early summer the Company had been forced to increase Third Class fares from 1d to 1½d per mile – but only to places where there was no competition! A 50% increase was a swingeing one and caused real hardship. The battle continued for over 12 months until in November 1883 they agreed a truce 'and determined to abandon projects which were likely to damage the other'. The rise in fares seems to have had little impact on the numbers coming to Torquay. A contemporary newspaper report shows that the 'masses' were arriving much earlier than is usually thought:

> According to all accounts, there has never been so large an influx of visitors into Devonshire; notwithstanding the extraordinary efforts of the Directors of the East Coast lines to divert holiday traffic to the watering places in their territory. A very large contingent of the tourist class has reached Torquay, but their stay is very brief, as they simply remain a day or two and then move off to more distant points. Others 'wiser in their generation', make Torquay their 'holiday centre', from which they make pleasant excursions every day.

These were all clearly healthy visitors and not delicate invalids!

Torquay's neighbours were anxious not to be left behind in the 'popularity stakes'. In June 1880 the people of Dartmouth petitioned the Great Western demanding that the '*Double Dutchman* which leaves Paddington at 3 pm and runs only to Paignton should be extended to Dartmouth'. Although not in the timetable as such the train was obviously well-known to the locals. The people of Paignton were not happy with their rail service either; three years later there were complaints that only four trains a day left for London. Two of these were First and Second Class only while on the others were 'a lot of open Thirds with scarce a foot-warmer'. The station-yard held only 25 wagons and there was no waiting room for passengers!

Journalists of the day printed with relish stories which would emphasise the short-comings of the Company:

> To the long list of grievances which has been made out against the Great Western Railway is added another, and that is the high rate charged for fish. A gentleman was frequently in the habit of having a salmon sent up to him from Totnes but the cost of carriage was so excessive that he determined upon adopting another method of obtaining the fish. Accordingly he sent a messenger to Totnes. The salmon was purchased and brought to Newton by the man as part of his *impedimenta*. The result was that the man's fare to Totnes and back was less by as many pence than would have been charged for sending the salmon alone.[6]

The printing of trivia worthy of some of today's Press continued. When Mr Grierson, the manager of the Great Western, took a house in Torquay three years later the *Torquay Directory* returned to the attack, saying 'possibly during his residence here, he will be enabled to prove by personal experience the accuracy of complaints made recently'.

Blizzard Years, 1881 and 1891

In January 1881 there was an historic snowstorm. Some Torbay trains were 'broken up' at Exeter and passengers could go no further. Although the Brixham branch closed for 36 hours the major difficulty faced by the Great Western was the 'want of water'; there was a very serious water shortage which caused some panic in Plymouth and

Devonport after the leat from Dartmoor, then the only source of supply, froze and became blocked. Just ten years later there was a second, now sometimes called the Great Blizzard of 1891. At one time six trains were snowed up between Newton and Plymouth. It was 'found necessary to have two engines on each train and lower the iron guard attached to the engine to clear the snow from the metals as the trains proceeded'. Later in the week 1,200 men were involved in clearing the line between Brent and Ivybridge. The *Flying Dutchman* was snowbound at Tiverton whilst the *Zulu* was halted at Taunton. The editor of the *Torquay Times* was one of those forced to take shelter in the town; he graphically described his experiences of a journey 'with plenty of promises but no footwarmers'. His journey from Bristol to Torquay took 24 hours – an experience not very different from those travellers from Newcastle to Plymouth during the more recent freeze-up of 1986/7. Delays on the Kingswear branch were described as 'comparatively trifling' but a large tree fell across the line near Torre Station and 'there was a narrow escape of the train being thrown off the line in consequence'.

The decade closed with two more minor accidents, fortunately without causing any injuries. In 1885 the engine of the 4.15 pm up-train came off the rails just outside the station and fell down a 6 foot bank. Four years later, at Dainton, a serious case of vandalism, worthy of the twentieth century, occurred. Three large stones, each weighing over a hundredweight, were placed on the lines deliberately. They were hit by the 'pilot engine [which] was ahead of the express otherwise a serious accident would have resulted'.

Travelling in the dark had improved when rape-oil roof lamps were introduced but the arrival of gas lighting in 1882 was a major innovation, particularly when the account is read of the arrival of the Plymouth express *Zulu* at Exeter in 1889 – the first time portable gas had been seen in the West Country. New carriages had 'an "illuminant" which shewed off to advantage the elaborate decorations of the coaches. The officials do not appear to have had a hint beforehand of the intended change, for on arrival of the train at that station, the lamp-men were fully prepared to put the usual oil lamps in the carriages but much to their surprise their services were not required'.

Gas remained the sole medium of lighting until electricity began to replace it early this century; it was not however finally ousted until the last old carriages were scrapped after World War Two.

The Great Western was facing a much more serious problem than lighting and heating their trains. Critics had quickly recognised that the Broad Gauge was an anachronism in the nation's railway systems. As early as 1848 a local newspaper had printed an extract from Robert Stephenson and Lock's Report that 'the London & South Western Railway trains on the standard gauge travelled at a higher rate of speed (by 1½ miles per hour) than those of the GWR from London to Exeter on the broad gauge'.[7] Whilst this was soon disproved, the broad gauge always had more detractors than supporters. Within ten years one of the GWR's own share-holders was proposing that 'the broad gauge should all be torn up', but he was shouted down.[8] Moreover the first conversions had taken place as early as the 1860s. By 1890 its last stronghold was in the south-west.

In 1891 Torquay, then at the height of its popularity with the Victorians, was brought within five hours running time of London for the first time. This was still of course on the 'long' route through Swindon and Bristol; the trains were broad gauge but the track over which they ran was for the most part 'mixed', a third line being laid at the standard width within the old seven feet of Brunel's. West of Exeter, with the exception of some miles in West Cornwall, it was all the latter. It was therefore no surprise when, later in the year, a notice was issued: 'The directors have come to the conclusion that the entire discontinuance of the broad gauge is unavoidable and the conversion of the railways of the Company in the West of England cannot longer be postponed without detriment to the interests of the Company, and have determined to carry out the conversion in the Spring of 1892'. There were some 170 miles of broad gauge track spread over Devon and Cornwall between Exeter and Truro, and of course down to Kingswear and on the other local branch lines as well.

From Broad to Standard Gauge in the West.

It was determined to carry out the whole operation over one weekend in May 1892 and elaborate preparations were made at Paddington by the Company; amongst them a detailed 50-page manual of instructions on the *modus operandi*. At ground level nuts and tie-bolts were thoroughly oiled, rails measured and alternate cross-members cut. A local newspaper forecast: 'We are to return to the coaching days. To the lovers of the quaint and picturesque the pity of it is that the revival will only extend for a couple of days during which the Great Western broad gauge is to be converted in to the narrow ... [As well as the suspension of freight and other services] people must unmurmuringly accept a diminished postal service'. On Thursday 19 May special trains were run conveying permanent-way men and others from all parts of the system. They were dropped in parties of 60 at appointed places: each gang of 20 men working under their own ganger. The following day, Friday the 20th, the last broad-gauge train left Paddington pulled by *Great Western*; over a thousand saw her off. The *Torquay Directory* carried a banner headline 'The Broad Gauge is dead and the face of the West shall know it no more'. It described how a score of persons stood on Torre Station between eleven and twelve on Friday night. The train arrived from Kingskerswell and a knot of enthusiastic travellers struck up *Auld Lang Syne*; the driver was entreated to 'be careful'. With whistle blowing the train set off on its last journey to Kingswear to the sound of Three Cheers which could be heard all over the Valley. Some paid the surcharge so that they could keep their tickets but found that they had been post-dated 'May 21st' – the day the broad gauge was but was not! Those scenes were to be re-enacted half a century later during the Beeching era.

Early next morning the men started work, having been accommodated in station buildings and in tents pitched beside the line, some 70 men being billeted in the Goods Shed at Torre. So many men were involved that they could not be fed communally so the GWR provided cooking utensils, oatmeal gruel and sugar. Wills of Bristol gave every man two ounces of tobacco. Alcoholic drinks were absolutely forbidden. During the change-over passengers for Exeter were taken in the *Duchess of Devonshire* to Exmouth from whence they were taken on

The last broad gauge train leaves Torquay Station
(From a contemporary 3 inch-square slide)

Preparing for the gauge change, Teignmouth - May 1892

Torre Station, broad gauge station - 20 May 1892

Torre Station, standard gauge station - 23 May 1892
(Photographs taken there by Stephen Bretton; reproduced with the permission of his grand-daughter Mary)

Preparing for the gauge change, Torquay - May 1892

Torquay Station photographed from the same spot - May 1987

London & South Western Railway trains to Exeter. First thing on Monday morning standard-gauge trains were running throughout the West Country.

The cost of conversion was said to be half a million pounds, of which rolling stock accounted for £375,000 (200 engines, of which 67 were broken up; 552 carriages, of which only 12 went out of use, and 3,269 trucks, of which 2,477 were condemned). It was reported that: 'To replace the locomotives 21 new ones are nearing completion at Swindon whilst the new carriages will have electric communication with the guard by means of buttons in each compartment but a passenger in distress will be able, by pulling the present cord outside the window, actually to put on the brake and stop the train'. By first thing on Monday the first standard gauge trains were running in the south-west. New express trains from Paddington to Torquay were introduced almost immediately. There was one unfortunate casualty. On 25 May, an inquest was held on James Webber of Rosary Road, Torquay, a ganger who had committed suicide – he was afraid that he would not have enough tools for the special contingent of men sent down. He was continuously thinking and talking about the two and a quarter miles of line for which he was responsible, being anxious whether 'it would turn out alright'. He had apparently walked into the sea and his body had been found on Hollacombe Beach.

Sixty years of continuous service followed when the millions of holidaymakers who came by train brought wealth and prosperity to the 'English Riviera'.

VIII THIRTY YEARS OF PROGRESS

Into the Twentieth Century

A newspaper announced on 2 July 1892 that the first through carriages were arriving in South Devon from Liverpool. It is a delight to find a contemporary description of such a journey made only a few months later. In November, Isabella and Jean Cowan, two young Americans in their twenties, arrived on the liner *City of New York*. *Aunt Belle's Diary* has only recently been published[1] and gives, in its early pages, the couple's experiences as they journeyed south:

> We traveled 2nd class from Liverpool to Torquay; a distance of 305 miles for $9.50 cents in 8 hours and 30 minutes. We were very disappointed with English travel accommodations. All the arrangements are so different, that we were two or three hours enroute before we felt at ease. I had often heard of English cars being divided into apartments [compartments], but I was not prepared to be quite as shut up as we were. Our apartment was about 5 feet wide. Its one long seat, placed so that we rode backwards, was much more comfortable than its rather shabby appearance promised. At each end of the tiny room was one small fixed window. A door opened out at each end of the tiny room, between the window and the opposite wall. At first we wondered how summer travelers managed to exist, without the least provision for fresh air. Presently we discovered that the upper half of each door serves also as a window which can be lowered provided one learns how it is done. Partly by experiment and partly by observation, we learned how to manipulate the clumsey leather strap, that is, at once, catcher and roller.

Corridor coaches date from the 1890s, about the time steam heating in winter was coming into use. The latter had not reached Devon, because Aunt Belle continues: 'Another peculiarity was their form of heating. This was done at all seasons by nothing more complicated than tin flasks of hot water. As they are re-filled quite frequently, it is wonderful how warm one keeps, if protected by a reasonable amount of wraps'. They were still in use on West Country trains after 1900; the water being changed at Exeter and Bristol.

Aunt Belle was too early to enjoy meals on the train. Restaurant cars were introduced on two services in 1896. One of these was the Paddington to Plymouth but the car only accommodated 16 people and was available to First Class passengers only; a local newspaper complained bitterly: 'Do not Second and Third class passengers need to dine and lunch also?' It was not until 1902 that they could.[2] By the 1930s both the Cornish Riviera and the Torbay Express had seating for 24 First Class and 64 Third Class at each sitting. The conditions under which the staff worked may be judged from 'the kitchen of the Cornish Riviera express is 10ft long and 6ft. 6in. wide, less area than is given in the kitchen of an ordinary suburban villa'. The passing of the conductor down the train offering reservations for 'First sitting for lunch' or 'Second sitting for dinner' seems to have continued until the very recent past!

In spite of the improvements which had followed the gauge-change the desire to 'put Torbay on the main line' remained; in April 1894 the Totnes, Paignton and Torquay Railway Bill went before Parliament but was not passed. The matter was revived three years later, again without success, as not unnaturally the GWR vigorously opposed the scheme. The subject was revived yet again in the 1920s, still without any success.

Just before the new century dawned, in June 1899, the Great Western introduced its second fastest train. This was the Torquay to London Express; just 50 minutes to Exeter then 'expressed non-stop to Paddington' in 3 hours 50 mins, via Bristol of course. This was a saving of 40 minutes on the old *Torquay Express* (the name first appeared in the timetable in June 1892.) At the other end of the market the Company introduced steam rail-motors. These were first introduced between Stonehouse and Chalfont in 1903; they must have appeared in the West Country soon after – an early picture postcard shows one arriving at Dawlish Warren with the destination 'Teignmouth' on its roller-indicator. According to the *Torquay Directory* they were used on the Kingswear branch from November 1910. They were finally phased out by the Company in 1935. Later, most of the coach portions were altered to motor rail use but retained their gas lighting.

Newton Abbot had the rare opportunity of welcoming Royalty in July 1899. The Duke and Duchess of York, later King George V and Queen Mary, arrived there by special train on their way to stay with Lord and Lady Clifford at Ugbrooke. They were met with great pomp when, as well as making a speech, the Duke inspected a guard of honour 'set up outside the arrival platform'.

In a recently published history[3] Robin Stanes writes: 'It is unlikely that tourism could ever have developed the way it did without the railways. Dawlish, Exmouth, Sidmouth and Torbay were already exclusive resorts for the well-to-do and elegant terraces and villas had been built ... But the railways opened Devon up to the less well-off. Fares to Ilfracombe were set deliberately high to deter those working people who could afford a holiday'. Day-trippers were not welcomed everywhere in South Devon either. When an enquiry was sent out early this century at Teignmouth, a controversy raged as to whether they should be encouraged or not. One official felt that they should be banned; other complaints concerned their drunkenness in the street. The general verdict however, was that they were not detrimental to the welfare of the town – and in any case local tradesmen profited from them considerably.

Excursionists from the North.
This does not seem to have been the attitude to day visitors in Torbay. The standard gauge link to the north made possible the visit of the 'Rochdale excursionists' to Torbay. Arranged by the Rochdale Merchants and Trademen's Association in July 1897, it brought 3,000 in six special trains, the first of which was timed to arrive at 7.25 am, the last at 9.40. Another 2,000 came in two special trains from Devonport. About two-thirds of the Northerners and all the Devonport excursion-

An 11-coach train leaving Dawlish Station, early 1900s

ists left the same night. Bank holidays then were not all that could be desired as 'a stiff breeze blew out many of the fairy lights almost as soon as they were lighted. The fine festoons of Japanese lanterns swung high above the pier and burned steadily with splendid effect'. This was before electric light was generally in use and therefore the candles, hundreds of them, were all lighted individually. The whole event was repeated two years later when 2,500 arrived in seven special trains. Most were again in the town for just one day though '200 had purchased 16-day and 500 eight-day tickets'. Unfortunately the day-trippers were 'unable to view the illumination of the Princess Gardens, put on by the Council for the excursion. Owing to the high winds, the majority of the fairy lights could either not be lit, or were blown out. The first return trains left at 4 pm; the last at 8.20 – the guests having all enjoyed 9 hours in Torquay'. These numbers pouring into the towns must have taxed everybody's resources – some managed to reach Brixham by steamer; others took the omnibuses and waggonettes which lined up outside Torquay Station as the trains arrived. How the limited numbers of eating places coped with them was barely mentioned in the newspapers; obviously they coped with the influx somehow.

The Torbay Towns Greet the Twentieth Century

Throughout the nineteenth century Torquay seems to have created its reputation without any extensive publicity though it benefited greatly from established guidebooks which eulogised its 'salubrity' and the 'equability of its climate', and from articles which appeared from time to time in the 'quality magazines' of the day. It could be said that these were read only by the upper and middle classes so it may be that when Torquay received its charter as a borough in 1892 it set out, whether deliberately or not, to attract additional visitors of all classes. In April 1900 its Council decided to advertise the town in the *Morning Leader* and other newspapers. Picture posters were however condemned as offering 'poor publicity'. Later it was to benefit from the superb GWR products which were displayed on almost every station in the system. In 1902 an information bureau for visitors was set up but it was 11 years before the 'official guide' arrived – a very modest affair compared with the glossy efforts of today. Right from the start the advantages of coming by train were stressed, as that very first guide shows. Possibly emulating Torquay, neighbouring towns (Teignmouth was one) were, within a year or so, following its lead and advertising too. Perhaps the most used publicity photograph of the time, popular for many years, was that of a Great Western express steaming at full speed beside the sea between Dawlish and Teignmouth. According to Frank Booker[4] the inspired slogan *The Holiday Line* was coined in 1903 and by brilliant and sustained advertising the Company prospered like the resorts it served.

Paignton too was expanding and deserved a better station, so in 1903 the down platform was widened and fitted up with a waiting-room. The improved booking facilites also permitted cheap day tickets to be issued there for the first time; as noted above, until then intending travellers had to go to Torquay for them!

In 1902 King Edward VII and Queen Alexandra travelled by Royal

Platforms at Paignton, the 'up', late 1890s

Platforms at Paignton, the 'down', late 1890s

Train to Kingswear to lay the foundation stone for the new naval college at Dartmouth, now best known as BRNC or 'Britannia'. Appropriately the Train was drawn by *Britannia*, and it set a non-stop record by covering the 229 miles between London, Bristol and Kingswear in 4 hours 23 minutes. After the College's opening in 1905 generations of future Royal Navy officers, including Royal princes, had their first glimpse of the magnificent building on Mount Boone from the window of a GWR railway carriage, having travelled from Paddington in the special train. One of those first cadets wrote:[5]

> The railway siding opposite our mooring was called Britannia Siding and was used by officers and cadets only; the train being halted there for them if requested to do so.

Later Britannia Halt was built beside the ferry slipway. This was done when the old wooden-walls *Britannia* and *Hindustan* were still in use. *Britannia* had, of course, arrived on the River Dart in the same year as the completed line to Kingswear.

The effects of erosion have changed the coastline of Devon radically over the centuries. Within Torbay a landslip occurred at Hollacombe in February 1903. Mr Bonning, described in the *Torquay Times* as an 'old employee', was on duty near the tunnel when he

> detected a subsidence in progress. He placed detonators on the line from Paignton and set off to stop the 10.49 pm from Torquay. The margin of time at the disposal of Bonning was short and it was shortened even more by his fall, in the darkness, into the fissure by the line which the landslide had created. He managed to scramble out however and proceeding as fast as his legs could carry him, he entered the tunnel. In the tunnel he could hear the noise of the train which had just left Torquay and had only just emerged from the tunnel when he saw the train approaching. By vigorously waving his red light, shouting and placing detonators on the line the plucky fellow succeeded in arresting the attention of the driver, and preventing the train, with its occupants rushing to possible disaster.

Train emerging from Breakneck Tunnel, Livermead, early 1890s

Opening out Breakneck Tunnel at Livermead, c.1908

GWR Motor Buses Introduced into Devon

That same year (1903), the Great Western saw the possibilities of using motor buses as 'feeders' to their stations, the first vehicles rattling their way from Helston to the Lizard. A little over a year later two appeared in Torbay. Steam buses were in vogue at the time but the GWR's were petrol-driven. There was one double-decker, which carried 18 inside and 20 on top; the other was a single-decker, similar in appearance to the old horse-wagonettes, with room on the roof for luggage, open sides with waterproof curtains and longitudinal seats for 20 people. It had the Cornish registration number *AF 203* which would suggest that it had been used on the Lizard service. Both buses seem to have had 20 h.p. engines and were equipped with solid india-rubber tyres. The service was half-hourly 'when both ran' and the fare for the full journey was 4d (less than 2p). The original pair were soon replaced with improved double-deckers. There were some problems with the brakes; on the steep hill at Livermead (the tunnel was then still there) passengers were sometimes required to walk while the conductor, who was equipped with a triangular chock, walked beside the vehicle, ready to thrust it under the back-wheel if it began to run backwards. Nevertheless there was concern that the buses were going too fast in Paignton so the Company issued 'strict orders to drivers to avoid going through the Town at an excessive speed and have care in going round corners'. In April 1905 the Paignton to Totnes service was inaugurated; one of the Milnes-Daimlers which ran was of an unusual design, it was part saloon and part observation coach. Over the years the Company's fleet became based at Paignton and remained in operation until January 1929, following the Great Western Railway (Road Transport) Act 1928, an agreement between the Great Western Railway and the National Bus Company brought Western National buses into the town.

The Last Bottle-neck between Dawlish and Teignmouth is Removed

The Great Western's concern for its West Country services generally must not be forgotten. The part of the line between Parson's Tunnel and Teignmouth had been doubled as long ago as 1884 (when the

GWR buses and their drivers line up at Paignton, c.1904

GWR double-decker bus at Torquay (probably in 1904)

tunnel east of the station there was opened out), leaving just a mile and a half through the tunnels as single track. This, and other single sections on busy routes, continued to cause delays, as trains could only pass over them using the 'single staff', which was essential for safe working. The development and introduction of the 'electrical staff' in 1891, enabled trains to be worked safely from either end. Not surprisingly, the first place chosen by the GWR for its adoption was between Dawlish and Parson's Tunnel. This single line continued to restrict services for more than 10 years, until in conjunction with the building of new seawalls, the tunnels were widened for double tracks (while the trains kept running – thanks to the generous dimensions required by the broad gauge), the work being completed in two stages, in June and October 1905. The view south-west from Dawlish has changed little since. Less than a year later the opening of the line from Reading to Taunton via Westbury, (when the Castle Cary-Langport section was completed in 1906), reduced the journey-times of expresses to the West Country dramatically (it was 20 miles shorter than the Bristol route). It was now possible to travel by express from Paddington to Torquay in 3 hours 50 minutes!

Crossing the Dart.

Down on the River Dart 1908 saw the arrival of the GWR vessel, which was to become familiar to thousands, when the *Mew* replaced the *Dolphin*. The *Dolphin* was originally built in 1869 by Harvey of Hayle and was authorised by the then Board of Trade to carry 331 passengers. In March 1902 her deck cabin was specially and luxuriously furnished to carry the King and Queen when they made their Dartmouth visit. The *Mew* was a screw-propelled vessel registered to carry 547 passengers, which gives some idea of the numbers using the railway at the beginning of the century.[6] She was built by Cox of Falmouth and remained in service until broken up in 1955. At the time of the evacuation of the BEF from Dunkirk (1940) she struggled along the coast to Dover but was considered unsuitable for use on the beaches. Finally considered 'worn-out',she was in turn replaced by the diesel ferries *Humphrey Gilbert* and *Adrian Gilbert*, but with the end of BR's operations they were both sold. They are now both back in the River on ferry duties.

Dolphin *moored at pontoon, Dartmouth, early 1900s*
(Note new embankment has been built)

Double tracks had been put down as far as Torquay in the 1870s, but it took over 30 years for them to be extended the further three miles to Paignton. The work finally started in 1909 and was completed late in 1910 at an estimated cost of £20,000 by Relf of Plymouth. This necessitated the opening out of Breakneck tunnel (the wall on one side can still be seen from the upper deck of a Torquay-Paignton service bus), surplus soil being taken to Newton Abbot and dumped beside the line to Moretonhampstead, where the new goods shed was later built. As the work progressed observers with long memories commented that 'the steam navvy filled a truck with a few scoops' – all very different from the way the original route had been hewn out laboriously by hand. In spite of the work 43 trains a day continued to run, equivalent to one every 20 minutes between 9 am and 9 pm.

Feelings against Bournemouth were still running high at this time; a prominent Torquay citizen protested: '*they* had four trains a day from the North, not just carriages'. Torbay demanded something similar and took its demands direct to the General Manager himself, with no effect.

116

Perhaps as a sign of changing times the Great Western Railway abandoned Second Class in October 1910. Up to this time *nine* different types of accommodation were required on long-distance trains: Smoking, Non-Smoking and Ladies only, in each of the three classes. One reformer said that it marked the 'final triumph for the third-class passenger'. Both classes of accommodation were to be used to the full in West Country trains for the next 40 years.

Dawlish Warren – Destination for Day-trippers.

Facing eastwards towards the open sea, the coast around Dawlish Warren has suffered from attack by the waves for centuries. Before the railway came, Langstone Rock was a prominent headland with fields right up to the edge of a sheer cliff. The South Devon Railway changed all that. Its line cut through the arable land, and the solid embankment wall, which it built to the south-west, protected the cliffs which until then had 'fed' the beach with soil and rocks. The erosion, to which the coast was always subject, worsened. As an 1860 *Guidebook* explained, the Warren at that time extended 'upward of 2 miles along which is the road to the Ferry Boat at Exmouth, the property of the South Devon Railway'. The Company had acquired much of the land from Exeter City Corporation, and with it the on-going cost of keeping the waters at bay!

Perhaps with this in mind the GWR, as successors to the SDR, felt obliged to encourage day-trippers to make full use of the place, so Dawlish Warren Halt was opened in 1905: it became a manned station in 1912. It was particularly popular with Exeter people who flocked there in the steam rail-motors; contemporary photographs show an additional carriage or two was often attached to increase the numbers carried.

In the early 1920s the area was saved from destruction by the Great Western, which built an embankment about 300 yards long at high-water mark. It was originally faced with piles and tied together with old rails, but subsequently the Company extended it and was forced to protect it even further by tipping huge boulders to form a crude but effective breakwater. This work continued from time to time and in the fifties British Railways continued the defensive works using, among other methods, rail and sleeper barriers until in 1959 the Warren passed into the control of the Local Authority. Until then there was a siding from the main line on the down side.

In March 1936 Camp Coach Holidays were introduced – accommodation for 6, 8, or 10 people was offered; there were living and dining sections and a 'galley' for preparing meals. Initially in Devon they were on offer at Ashton, Avonwick, Dawlish Warren, East Anstey, Ide, Lustleigh and Thorverton. Those 'retired' cream and brown carriages have stood at the Warren for most of the years since then. Still popular with holidaymakers they are now 'privatised'. The Teign Valley locations were in use until the line closed.[7]

Another little-known project in the area designed to take beach-goers nearer the sands was Preston Platform, midway between Torquay and Paignton, which opened for the first time in July 1911 (It closed shortly after the outbreak of the 1914-18 War and never reopened). By the 1960s all that could be seen were the platform corner-stones on the down side.

Although two major strikes affecting the railway took place after the 1914-18 War, there was a coal strike during Easter 1912 which led to 28 of the 62 trains due to run from Torbay being cancelled. Travellers must have been severely inconvenienced; it must be remembered that working people then had only the Easter, Whitsun and August Bank Holiday weekends to take a short break from work-bench, shop counter or office desk. It was perhaps the only opportunity they would have in that year and the failure to return on time would have had serious consequences too. Recalling this strike an old railwayman has said that this was the first failure in reliability by the railways, and was one of the factors which led to its decline half a century later.

What appeared to be a great innovation for ordinary folk travelling to the West Country was the *Devon and Cornwall Special* introduced in 1913 – it carried passengers for Paignton as well as Newquay and Falmouth and was Third Class only. It had a restaurant car, bicycle stands and reserved seats. Reserved seats were a GWR innovation too; they had been allowed on the *Cornish Riviera* for the first time in 1905.

The attraction of the Whitsun holiday for working people can be found in the description of the weekend excursion from London in

1913. The *Daily News & Leader* organised a 'special non-stop, numbered-seat excursion from London to Torquay'. Five hundred people travelled, out of the 624 provided for. The fare for the weekend was 17/-d [85p]. The train consisted of 'ten claret-coloured corridor coaches, and was drawn by the giant engine *King James*. The journey of 199½ miles took 207½ minutes. One passenger spent much of his leisure timing the train by means of a stop-watch and the quarter-mile posts by the track ... Hundreds of persons awaited the arrival of the train. They lined the bridges on each side of Torquay Station and thronged the exit'. As noted later the arrival of holiday trains were to fascinate local people for many years to come! Some years earlier there was a half-day excursion to the Nelson Centenary Carnival at Alexandra Palace which left South Devon around noon and cost just 6/6d [33p] – an amount within the pockets of many ordinary folk.

A few months later, August Bank Holiday prompted a Torquay journalist to write: 'The town has been invaded as it has never been invaded before; it began on Friday while Saturday's arrivals have been enormous. Streams of people pour along the Torbay Road all day from the earliest morning until late at night. Those who have not booked accommodation search for apartments – the unsuccessful ones returning to the station to hie off elsewhere'. This was a foretaste of 'things to come', but not for some time. Within a year all Europe was at war and holidays by the seaside were forgotten.

Joint rail-road outings to Dartmoor later became more popular although they were on offer throughout the pre-War period. At first horse-drawn wagonettes met the trains at Bovey Tracey and elsewhere; these were replaced in due course by motor charabancs, but these too ceased operating for the duration of the War.

As part of a major development scheme by the Company, the Great Western submitted a Bill to Parliament in December 1913. This included the building of the Aller loops[8] which were to be built on either side of the Torquay Branch near the junction with the Plymouth line. Like the holiday plans of the people these too were abandoned: post-War financial problems ensured that the scheme would never be started. The holidaymakers, however, were soon coming back in even larger numbers.

IX TWO WORLD WARS AND THE YEARS BETWEEN

The Big Four Created

During the 1914-18 War the Great Western Railway was deeply committed to the war effort. With all the other Companies it was taken over and remained under government control until 1921. The crippling casualties suffered by the Allies meant that the GWR ran over 6,000 fully-loaded hospital trains.[1] Patients were delivered to over 40 stations, including Paignton. The trains started arriving at the Station in 1914 with casualties on their way to the American Women's War Hospital at Oldway Mansion. They were taken there in buses belonging to the GWR and other operators. Arrivals took place at all hours of the day and night, when the volunteer stretcher parties included firemen and railwaymen. When the Somme offensive started in 1916 there were 255 beds available. Other hospitals were also set up in Torquay Town Hall and in the fine houses of the gentry. Torquay's *Record of the War* recorded the arrival of 154 hospital trains over the four years and said that 10,441 sick and wounded soldiers were distributed to the various establishments. It must be assumed that these did not include the Paignton arrivals.

By the time the war ended in 1918, considerable investment was needed to bring the services back to pre-War standards. There were social factors to be taken into account too. There was a short strike in 1919 which had resulted in all railwaymen getting rises in wages: although coal and other goods had gone up in price over the previous five years, there had been no increase in freight rates. The government of the day had to do something. It agreed to a massive reorganisation by passing the Railways Act in 1921, which created the 'Big Four'. It

'Box Brownie' snap of war-wounded arriving at Paignton, probably 1914

was perhaps appropriate that the only company not changing its name was the Great Western Railway, a name which had been in continuous existence since 1835.

In the following years the GWR had to face serious competition from road-hauliers, who had been able to buy secondhand war vehicles cheaply and in large numbers. This had a dramatic effect in reducing the volume of goods carried by rail but seems to have had little effect locally – where all the efforts were concentrated on improving services for passengers. One of the first tasks undertaken was the rebuilding of Newton Abbot Station. The reconstruction of the old and draughty Victorian relic was completed in April 1928, with two island platforms and imposing entrance and offices. Scissor cross-overs were installed so that the Torbay portions could be easily attached and detached from main line expresses. This ritual continued for 40 years, usually in the centre of Platform 1, where young passengers watched, as they quickly ran between carriage windows, in the hope that the 'Kingswear' would be signalled off before the 'Plymouth'. This was possible because, at the same time, the section to Aller had been rearranged as a four track section with the 'down' to Kingskerswell hard against the high wall, which was the boundary between road and rail at this point. ('Torquay portions' were finally abandoned in 1978). There were improvements at Kingswear about the same time.

There was a flourishing freight traffic too. Most of London's milk came from the West Country; Brixham fish went to Billingsgate and elsewhere, and there was seasonal produce and livestock from Devon farms. Ashburton during the Fair was said to be chaotic with rows of cattle trucks, shouting drovers and lowing cattle filling the station yard. One reporter found that passenger trains were being terminated at Buckfastleigh at Fair time! As well as local manufactured products, paper was still being made in large quantities at Buckfastleigh and Ashprington; all was carried out of Devon by train.

Within a few years of the War's end, holiday traffic had resumed and the enthusiasm for the seaside brought thousands to South Devon. The August Bank Holiday weekend of 1923 saw between 11,000 and 12,000 passengers leaving Paddington on the Friday afternoon alone, whilst over the weekend equally large numbers left Exeter for the coast:

2,000 to Dawlish Warren
1,000 to Dawlish
2,300 to Teignmouth
1,200 to Torquay

In addition 850 booked to Newton Abbot, no doubt *en route* to Dartmoor, but they did not join the 'Moor Train' from Dartmouth; this was advertised in Torbay as being 'non-stop to the Moreton branch'.

'Works outings' are as old as the railways! John Heathcoats of Tiverton (the lace-makers) brought its factory day trip to Teignmouth on 10 May 1854. Much later the GWR Swindon Works sent great numbers into all the South Devon coastal towns for their annual holidays in the early 1920s. Teignmouth particularly prospered from the trade these workers brought. Many travelled a little further; for example, between 1,500 and 1,800 came to Torquay in 1923 in two special trains – one Railway Company official forecast that the town would 'become the Brighton of the West'.

The importance which the Great Western attached to its West Country traffic led, with other publicity such as the posters mentioned earlier, to the publication of *Devon; the Shire of the Sea Kings*, written in a most flowery style. Very popular, it went through a number of editions. One, dated 1926, lists the Road Motor Car Services then operating. These were: Kingsbridge and Salcombe; Kingsbridge – Modbury, Yealmpton and Plymouth; Kingsbridge – Torcross and Dartmouth; Moretonhampstead and Chagford and Paignton and Totnes. It also offered Tours by Observation Cars from Bovey and Moretonhampstead Stations to Princetown and Tavistock; Bovey to Haytor Rocks and Bovey to Grimspound and Widecombe-in-the-Moor; thus offering itself as 'the natural key to all that is most beautiful and curious in Dartmoor'. A contemporary photograph shows that the old AEC solid-tyred charabancs were still predominant, but that a newer, more up-to-date Burford vehicle, with pneumatics, had arrived. The old charabancs had their problems on the steep hills up to the Moor and there are personal memories of passengers walking beside the struggling vehicle, the only persons remaining aboard being the driver and the infirm.

Another popular publication of the Company was the annual *Holiday Haunts*. This had started as early as 1904 and whilst not limited to the West Country, great prominence was given to the area. By the 1930s it contained well over a thousand pages.[2] There was even a 'utility' edition during World War Two.

A New Express for Torquay.

The name *Torquay Express* first appeared in timetables in 1892 but nothing appeared externally on the carriages. Although express trains continued to run for the next 30 years it was not until June 1923 that the GWR announced the introduction of a new service to the town with the title *Torbay Express*. This left Paddington at 12 noon each weekday, covering the 200 miles in just 215 minutes! (The non-stop train in the other direction left Torquay at 12.10pm). By 1925, when it made its magnificent run with 13 carriages the head-boards on each gave the title as *Torbay Limited*, the name by which it was more popularly known.[3] The engine head-board *Torbay Express* was introduced some years later. (British Rail dropped the name in 1965 but it has re-appeared on an Intercity 125 service to London again recently). In 1941, after the 'Battle of Britain' had been won, war-weary Londoners were given a chance to see the sea. The *Torbay Limited* ran for just five weeks in July and August. In the immediate post-war years, after the train had reached Kingswear, the engine was returned to Newton Abbot sheds overnight, leaving the chocolate and cream carriges on a siding beside the Dart, looking in the evening sun like some giant and somnambulant snake.

At the beginning of 1926 there was a great furore among holiday resorts when it was reported in the national newspapers that Torquay Town Council was to introduce a Visitors' Tax. It coincided with a request to the Great Western that the *Torbay Limited* should leave at eleven instead of twelve noon, as it was thought the revised time would be more convenient to travellers; exactly why was not fully explained. A deputation of local dignitaries were therefore dispatched 'to wait upon representatives of the GWR at Torquay Railway Station'. It was pointed out in local newspapers that much use had been made 'of the ill-timed proposal by various newspapers in the north, particularly those connected with rival resorts'. The name Blackpool was mentioned in one. Mr Nichols, the Superintendent of the Line, declared the scheme 'retrograde in the extreme, and one which should not for a moment be tolerated by such a progressive town and health resort as Torquay and therefore the GWR would oppose any Bill to Parliament to the utmost of its power'. A month later an ambiguously worded resolution was officially approved by the Council which killed the idea – just as it had been in 1907 when the ridiculous idea was first mooted. The timetable remained unchanged too!

In March 1928 Paignton Town Council made its last major purchase of land at Goodrington and almost immediately the Great Western suggested a station there. Working quickly the Company were able to open Goodrington Sands Halt in July. Before it closed for the winter many thousands had enjoyed the day there, although there were then few attractions except the smooth red sands. It opened again on 29

March 1929 – possibly an indication of the long season which Torbay then enjoyed. There was another 'new station' nearby; Broadsands Halt opened for excursion traffic on 9 July 1928. It was never in the timetable and was only used until September 1929.

In 1929 the *Torquay Pullman* was inaugurated. It was an eight-coach train with an interior decor in green and blue, and a capacity of 260 passengers. The initial publicity expressed the hope that the 'additional comfort and facilities will obviously make for a high class of visitor'. There were supplementary charges of 7/6d [38p] for First Class and 5/- [25p] for Third. It was however not a success, with only 24 passengers on the first run and so it was withdrawn at the end of the summer season a year later.

Whilst visitors to Torbay may not have patronised the Pullman they certainly stayed at the best hotels and one sign of their presence was the Private Bus Service from the station. Just as the hotels operated 'busses' to the Station in the 1840s, the appearance of small comfortable motor coaches 90 years later enabled a few of the premier Torquay hotels, including the Victoria & Albert and the Osborne, to offer a personal and private service of their own.

In an effort to help unemployment a large cash injection was made to the Big Four in 1929 of four and a half million pounds. Among smaller schemes proposed was a major one for Paignton and Goodrington. The platforms were lengthened by 120 feet and land was bought from Paignton for a goods shed and sidings for stabling trains. The work cost £30,000 and the goods depot came into use two years later. (Some years ago the whole property was sold, except some sidings, and has been replaced with residential flats). Torbay was enjoying immense popularity as a holiday centre so just four years later, in 1935, there were proposals for further expansion. There were to be more sidings and facilities behind Goodrington Sands (revived in 1956) and a new five-platform station at Paignton taking in part of Queen's Park. Later proposals included a dual-carriageway with a seven-span bridge at Roundham; in the end all that was done was the erection of the present steel-girder bridge there in 1939.

GWR Starts South Devon Air Service.

The GWR moved into air transport of freight and passengers when, in April 1933, an air service was inaugurated between Cardiff, Teignmouth, Torquay and Plymouth. After being suspended in the September, it resumed again in May 1934 under the name Railway Air Services Ltd (jointly owned by the four Companies and Imperial Airways); this operated from Plymouth to Liverpool, calling at Teignmouth (Haldon). The route-miles of this service quadrupled in three years.

An eagerly awaited sight, albeit only a brief one, was the passing of the boat-trains from Millbay to Paddington through Newton Abbot. Their coaches had unique and luxurious fittings, being specially built for the task at Swindon; local boys watching from the road nearby saw little of this splendour as the lightly-loaded trains steamed through at speed non-stop. About 500 vessels a year were calling at Plymouth in the mid-thirties.[4]

Circus on the Move.

The Victorians loved circuses. In their day it was Barnum and Bailey's and Bill Cody's Wild West Show; in the 1920s and 1930s Bertram Mills went on tour in a big way. They came to the West Country every three years and the railway played a large part in its transport. The 1933 arrival is recorded thus:[5]

> While residents and visitors slumbered, two long trains slid into Torquay Station. Hundreds of men appeared ... and the tremendous task of unloading commenced. The greater part of the equipment was carried on this train and the manner in which it is transported evokes deep admiration. Mr Mills has had fourteen road-rail trailers specially manufactured to his own specification. These are put on to low built trucks of considerable length and when these reach their destination they are taken off at the goods yard and are towed by tractors en route to the ground.
> It was not until several hours afterwards that the second train steamed in to an accompaniment of neighs and stamping of hooves. The animals have arrived and soon made the fact

known. Grooms and attendants embarked [sic] from the ordinary carriages in the front of the train and made their way to the different horse boxes. All the various animals in Bertram Mills' Circus possess their own individual type of wagon. The elephants travel in one of the longest vans on British railways. It is specially reinforced and is so roomy that in spite of the elephants' vast bulk they can move about among huge bales of straw. Each of the horses has its own stall, parts of which are lined with leather. A large crowd gathered to watch the elephants, horses, mules, zebras and ponies make their exits from the train and cross the road to the Recreation ground.

This was one rare occasion when the small sidings at Torquay were brought into use. Even then the electricity generators (in their famous red and green livery) and the performers came by road, the latter towing their residential caravans. The next place visited was Barnstaple where the same unloading procedure was followed.

GWR Excursions to the Channel Isles.

About every fortnight in those summer days when the sun always seemed to shine, the Great Western Railway ran their 'cheap-day trip excursions' to Guernsey and Jersey from Torquay harbour. The fare to Guernsey was 12/6 [63p] where the trippers had five hours ashore. It was more expensive on the longer Jersey voyage, 14/6 [73p].

Change-over day' is an ongoing phenomenon in holiday resorts, when in a few hours, in camps, flats, and boarding houses, inventories are checked and sheets changed between the time one week's holidaymakers leave and the new influx begins. In the years before, and immediately after, World War Two, on the GWR the weekly nightmare was known as 'Summer Saturdays'.[6] The problems of bringing thousands of tourists and dozens of trains through the bottleneck of Newton Abbot have been described in detail again recently.[7] Trains queued to enter the Kingswear branch and to go over Dainton to Plymouth and Cornwall; all stations, but particularly Torquay and Paignton, were extremely busy. People still arrived 'on spec', so there was some 'touting' for business by representatives from the smaller places which did 'B & B'. The medium-sized establishments, which called themselves 'hotels', were in such demand that they arranged 'meals only' for some guests – they returned to the dining room for breakfast after being accommodated some distance away in the spare bedrooms of neighbouring private houses.

Visitors Arrive in their Thousands.

In August 1933 a *Torquay Times* reporter joined the first arrivals at the station: 'The trek to Torquay started early on Saturday morning. Before two o'clock a train so long that it had to draw up twice at each of the stations at which it had stopped ... let loose the first wave of visitors. Another train arrived just before five in the morning containing "early-bird" holiday-makers who wandered around Torquay in the grey light of dawn, unwilling to worry the hotel or boarding house into which they had booked at that hour of the day'. The relationship between the increased popularity of the railways and the growth of inexpensive bed and breakfast in local private houses has still to be investigated. It is almost certain however that it was due to the demand by the rising artisan and working classes who were determined to come to the seaside even if their budgets were limited. There had been lodging houses for visitors from the late 1700s onwards; bed and breakfast, on the other hand, was a more recent innovation offered by part-time landladies in small domestic residences.

The first of the 'great seasons' seems to have been in 1936 when the stationmaster commented: '*If* there is good Torquay weather, the *Torbay Limited* will run in duplicate, even triplicate if necessary. There will be excursions from Leicester, Leeds, Manchester, Birmingham, the North and Wales. Then there will be the usual Londoners, whose numbers increase every year'. Come they did; almost over-night the population doubled – among the sights seen were passengers sleeping in the waiting room at Torquay Station, and others tramping up from the Strand at five o'clock in the morning waiting for lodging houses to open. Passengers were also making so much use of sleeping cars to the West Country that at times 'every available car was pressed into service'.

As the new industries developed and there was some rearmament following the rise of national socialism in Germany, and of fascism in Italy, factory workers, particularly from the Midlands and North, increasingly took their annual holidays in the south-west. A succession of departing trains 'banked up' the gradient from Torquay to Torre as they returned to these destinations – some of which ran non-stop out of Devon, so woe-betide anyone who boarded the wrong one in error! Most of the trains had at least a dozen coaches, others even more. (The modern Inter-City 125 has only seven which, even with today's reduced traffic, is not sufficient at busy times).

GWR buses about to leave Bovey Tracey for Dartmoor, c.1925

The out-going numbers almost matched those coming in but not quite! There was growing competition to the railways in the late thirties as motor coach services improved. Although much slower than holiday trains they were cheaper even then. As the trains were 'queuing up' to enter Torquay so too were the coaches, waiting to drop their passengers at Castle Circus Coach Station (all arrivals then came to what is now the car-park adjacent to Torquay Town Hall). The GWR was obviously aware of the competition but seemed to do little to combat it. After the end of World War Two in 1945 the same conditions prevailed for a few years but then the competition from the coaches was even greater.

For years local people gathered at vantage points, particularly on Chapel Hill overlooking the approach to Torquay and on the bridge to the north of Torquay Station to watch the continuous, or so it seemed, arrival of Saturday trains, headed by engines of all classes and with a wide variety of old and new rolling-stock. As at Torquay Station and elsewhere there was much activity at Torre too; visitors to St Marychurch and Babbacombe were encouraged to alight there. Many of the incoming services had to stop twice at the short down-platform. Impatient arrivals could be seen leaning out of carriage windows back beyond the Goods Shed (now a DIY warehouse) as they waited for the train to be moved forward to the accompaniment of much waving of arms and blowing of whistles. It all reached a climax in 1938 when on the August Bank Holiday weekend 20,000 people arrived in Torquay alone, of these 11,000 arrived on Saturday. On the Sunday, 50 excursions arrived from London, Wales. Bristol and the Midlands. It must be emphasised again that most of the trains used on weekend working had loadings of 11, 12 or 14 coaches, including the indispensable Restaurant Car. This meant there was seating for more than a thousand passengers, with all seats taken and more standing too! (As an indication of the decline in passenger traffic, compare these numbers with the 288 which can be accommodated in the 2nd Class accommodation on an Intercity 125 today). On the outward journey, except for the 'banker' (the smaller, usually a tank, engine, which provided additional power up the steep incline by pushing at the rear from Torquay to beyond Torre), the steam locomotives of the day covered the routes to London and South Wales without a change of engine. Trains for the Midlands went only as far as Bristol because from there the line was in the hands of another Company. Of course these halcyon days could not last; they did not: just a year later War seemed imminent and the Devon sands were soon being used to fill sandbags rather than make sand-castles.

Foreign royalty continued to arrive by train as they had done nearly a century earlier. In July 1933 King Feisal of Iraq 'stepped from a luxurious and special train' which had arrived 'on the stroke of time' at a station decorated with flags of the British Empire and he entered his Rolls-Royce landauette through an exit which was a 'mass of shrubbery'. After watching Fleet exercises he returned to his train through a huge crowd of admiring spectators. Nowadays celebrities use helicopters which are noisy, breezy and much less impressive.

The way west continued to be very important to GWR revenues, so plans were made to 'duplicate' the coastal section between the Exe and Teign Rivers. The proposed new line left the existing tracks midway between Starcross and Dawlish Warren, passing inland near Holcombe, and rejoining them at the head of the Estuary near Bishopsteignton. There were to be four tunnels and steepest gradient was 1:150. Land was bought in 1935 – but was sold off in the fifties when the need had gone.

The 'Ghost Train' on the Kingswear Branch.

Memories of the early 'runaway train' were recalled when, just before midnight, the 'Ghost Train' ran on the Kingswear branch. On 23 June 1937 an engine shedded at Newton Abbot 'thundered its way over the rails from the station past signal boxes and through three stations, minus driver and fireman, until it came to grief at catch-points near the Gasworks [between Torquay and Paignton]. It travelled with regulator and throttle fully open'.[8]

As the threat of war came closer, the Superintendent of the Line at Paddington assumed responsibility for Air Raid Precautions and through him detailed instructions were issued to every station in the system. The eight-page document for Torre Station has survived locally.[9] It covered every eventuality including a gas attack. An air-raid shelter was provided in the Goods Shed and the staff allocated to it were:

Torre Station Passenger staff	19
Goods Department Clerical Staff	13
Goods Department Wages Staff	39
Engineering Dept	7

This means that there were 78 people needed to run just one relatively small station; 40 years later there are none. Multiplied throughout the country it gives an indication of just how great the loss of jobs on the railway has been and how seriously areas like South Devon, where work opportunities are few, have suffered.

The Railways at War, 1939-1945.

Although many technical improvements were delayed or abandoned because of the War, one was allowed to be finished. In November 1939 the last ramp for the automatic train control was fixed at Penzance. It was an invention by members of GWR staff and had involved fitting 3,250 engines and laying down 2,114 ramps. A major safety device, it was the envy of the other Companies because it warned the driver of signals set against him. (Later, improvements to the system caused the brakes to be automatically applied when signals at danger were encountered).

After the fall of France there was a huge evacuation of women and children from London before and during the 'blitz'. Over 100,000 left in four days for the safer West Country. Early in 1941 the Army's Southern Command was allocated three armoured trains for Devon and Cornwall.[10] One was based at Newton Abbot for a time which operated between Exeter and Kingswear. Another was located at Barnstaple and this too made occasional runs as far as Newton Abbot; a third, based at Wadebridge, made at least one run to Newton Abbot. In April 1941 one of the trains was inspected at Newton Abbot by Lieutenant General (later Field Marshal Earl) Alexander. Their tasks were to engage ships, sea-planes and E-boats on the rivers Teign and Exe, and invading tanks on the beaches around Torbay. However a reorganisation left only one to cover the whole of Devon. The trains were withdrawn from operations in early 1943 when the LNER, which had supplied the locomotives, required additional engines urgently. Local railwaymen formed their own platoons of the Home Guard to protect their vital life-line from enemy interference.

The Royal Air Force arrived in Babbacombe round about Dunkirk time in June 1940. An Initial Training Wing (ITW) was set up, based at the Norcliffe Hotel; others followed in Torquay and Paignton (at Oldway). Their presence in Torbay ended shortly before D-day, by which time over 53,000 men had trained for air-crew duties – including some well-known aces of the time. Practically all these arrived and departed from the local stations – when men going on leave and on 'weekend passes' are added, the additional traffic generated must have put a severe strain on the railway's already stretched resources. There

A 1939/45 poster which discouraged rail travellers

was also an RAF rehabilitation centre at Torquay's Palace Hotel (until it was bombed in 1942); most of these badly-mutilated airmen would have been brought to Torquay Station. A United States Army hospital was built at Stover; the ambulance trains came down the Teign Valley line, always at night and without lights showing.[11]

On the whole South Devon was fortunate. Despite the frequent intrusions by German fighter-bombers, the only major damage suffered by the railway was at Newton Abbot. In August 1940 bombs hit the station and yard – 15 people were killed and others seriously injured.

In a story told elsewhere[12] the forces of the United States arrived in the south-west during the winter of 1943-4. To cater for the military trains required by the U.S. forces in the Heathfield area, loop lines were put in there and on the Teign Valley line to serve their stores on Knighton Heath.[13] Many thousands were in the area (quite apart from the South Hams battle area); how many of these here came as passengers by rail is not known but in the D-day operations a total of 3,035 special trains for troops, stores and equipment were run; in addition there were 167 trainloads of prisoners-of-war going away from the ports.[14]

Almost as soon as the troops and ships had set off for Normandy a civilian invasion of South Devon was imminent. The ban on movement to the coast was removed on 11 July 1944 and for the first time in five years the beaches of Torbay were open to visitors. 'We expect a big rush of holidaymakers to the South West', said the GWR. Because it was wartime there were no extra trains as London was still being menaced by the 'V' weapons. At one stage Paddington Station was so crowded, intending travellers were being advised to try the other London termini! The arrivals were able to use the beaches as it was also in July that the barbed-wire barriers were taken down from the promenades and beaches. Paignton Pier was unusable as a section had been removed after the fall of France to prevent it being used by invading Germans. There were other less willing arrivals by train at this time; over 2,000 evacuees had come into Paignton to escape the flying-bombs – they had been sent to other coast towns as well.

The peace in 1945 brought a change of government and the desire for railways and other industries to be owned by the people. In 1948 the railways were nationalised and **British Railways** was born.

X   DECLINE AND FALL

The immediate post-War years brought renewed prosperity to South Devon. Families had been separated and servicemen had returned with gratuities – money to be spent by some on seaside holidays. Former evacuees also returned to see the Devon people who had fostered them in the darkest days. The first peacetime Summer was 1946 but for victorious Britain it was a difficult time. Just before August Bank Holiday bread rationing began. Local bakers were concerned about the complexity of it all as 'there were seven categories of ration all on different pages of the Ration Book'. Some delivery-men were working until eight at night cutting out the little squares of card; the scheme they said would never work in a holiday town like Torquay with a floating population of many thousands. It did, of course, and it was really a tranquil Bank Holiday. Including day visitors there were 20,000 holiday-makers in the town: 'altogether 1,000 more people arrived at Torquay station over the weekend than in 1939, when it was estimated that 15,000 people passed through the barriers'. They only saw patched old flags flying; the material for making new ones was not available. 1947 saw the issue of the GWR's new Torquay poster, commissioned from a well-known artist. Unfortunately Torquay's Public Relations Committee did not like it, and as it had not been submitted to or approved by it, refused to make any contribution to the cost!

In 1948 the Olympic yachting events took place in Torbay. Many of the visitors who came to watch the vessels of the 25 nations taking part came by train – motor cars, like new flags, were in short supply. During the same year Bertram Mills' Circus resumed its visits to the south-west in much the same way as before the War. These continued at three year intervals until the 1960s.

Memories of food rationing may remain but the fuel crisis of 1952 is forgotten. Because of this the Brixham branch closed down completely but opened up again almost immediately. In July 10,000 passengers arrived in Torquay on one Saturday alone; those who were returning were given free boarding tickets which for the first time prevented departures from being too overcrowded.

How little things had apparently changed in a decade. August Bank Holiday 1954 was described as a 'raincoat and umbrella' weekend. About 12,000 came on the Saturday, most on the 14 extra trains, some of which arrived very early in the morning. A sea-front cafį opened at 3.30 am and had served 1,500 breakfasts by 9 am. Another, with a higher tariff, only served 750! Large numbers of visitors were still leaving at the start of the Weekend.

To meet the demand for increased railway facilities the Tanner's Bridge project was revived in 1955. The contract was signed with Staverton Builders to build a locomotive turn-table (65 feet in diameter), a water-tower, ash-pit, an engineers' and shedmens' cabin, and additional sidings on the landward side of Goodrington South Sands – when it came into operation a year later diesel power was already taking over. Only months later it was announced that the whole system west of Exeter would be diesel traction only. By the following February the bridge and steps were in position and the new Goodrington Station opened later in the year.

Although traffic was down from the pre-War peak of over 20,000, 16,433 passengers came in on a peak day in 1957. 83 engines were operating out of Newton sheds for all types of work and 41 went to the Kingswear branch for holiday working; this included 'double-heading' and 'bankers'. There were over 30 major departures from Torquay between early morning and mid-afternoon which taxed both station and operating staff. The following year (1958) numbers of passengers arriving in Torbay were again above average but down on the previous year, – the decline had started even though there were still bargains available. Mr Collins, the Torquay station-master, reminded residents and visitors alike that holiday runabout tickets – seven days unlimited

On the Kingsbridge Branch shortly before closure, Loddiswell

travel between Plymouth, Exeter and Exmouth – were good value at 18/6d [93p]. (One day out on the much more limited network now (1987) costs £3.50) Within ten years redundancies among all grades were well under way.

As explained earlier, the years 1958 and 1959 saw the closures of three Devon branch lines; the Brixham branch was to follow four years later. In June 1959 the *Meccano Magazine* (that wonderful toy later suffered a similar decline to the railways) included a short news-item that driverless trucks were being tried experimentally in the Newton Goods Shed. Using a guidance system under the floor, trolleys took loads of up to 3 tons between wagons and cartage vehicles – an indication of the volume of goods then going through. The success or otherwise of this particular piece of technology is not known but within ten years goods deliveries had declined considerably and Newton Abbot took responsibility for a wide area, being the only one open between Exeter and Plymouth; all operations at Paignton were also transferred there and deliveries were undertaken by National Carriers Ltd. There have been no goods handled there for some years and an attempt by a private individual to use the large shed as an entertainment centre has ended too. The rail link to Teignmouth Old Quay from the main line was taken up in 1968 after being in existence for over a century. This had been completed in 1851, barely five years after the railway arrived in the town. Following nationalisation British Railways discouraged freight on main-line sidings and so clay exports were transferred to road haulage; even then the track was left *in situ* for some years so that the link could be restored if the situation changed.[1]

The decline in the number of stations open for passengers has been less dramatic. Exminster closed in 1964, whilst between Newton Abbot and Plymouth all have gone except Totnes: Wrangaton, Bittaford, Ivybridge, Cornwood and Plympton shut in 1959: Brent followed in 1964. Twenty years on Totnes still survives. The recent innovation by BR which permits Dart Valley Railway trains into Totnes Station may prolong its life even longer. Exactly why it does remain is not clear. Bus services to the South Hams are inadequate, and to nearby Dartmoor no better! The major coach tour operators work through the town rather than from it.

Doubts about the viability of West Country branch lines were again expressed in 1960 and about that of the Kingswear branch in 1966. In 1967 a pious hope was voiced that local holiday resorts should invest to protect their lifelines; unfortunately those towns were not in any position to help! The next move came just before Christmas 1969 when the Government announced that it would provide £229,000 to bolster local services in South Devon.[2] The whole of the Exeter to Paignton local service would now be a 'branch line'. A result of this was that the Paignton to Kingswear section became a real 'backwoods' branch line with only one diesel unit going back and forth, except on Summer Saturdays when there were two through trains. One Kingswear train was scheduled to reach Paignton a few minutes after the 'connection' had left!

As 1971 drew to a close it was obvious that its days were numbered even though both Devon County Council and Torbay County Borough Council were now prepared to subsidise it for six months. The costs for

Lord Beeching sees off first DVR train at Buckfastleigh, May 1967 (South Devon News photograph)

139

Flying Scotsman *at Kingswear*
(Photo: M Hobson)

the coming year were estimated at £61,000 and, with income of only £14,000, there was little surprise when formal notice of closure was given in February 1972. This was followed on 10 March with the announcement that the Dart Valley Railway hoped to take over the line with effect from 1 August. Events moved quickly, on 16 March the British Railways Board (Paignton & Kingswear) Light Railway Order was published by the Department of the Environment. The Board had accepted the Dart Valley's offer of about £¼million; £25,000 would be spent on signalling and track alterations. The *DVR Magazine* explained that a considerable proportion of the purchase money would be recovered from the sale of surplus land at Goodrington and Kingswear. One of the first tasks to be tackled was the repainting of Kingswear Station which, it alleged, had not been done since the end of World War Two! Eventually it was announced that BR would cease to be responsible for the section after October 28 but that it would continue to run the railcar, four times a day, until the track alterations had been made. These continued until December 29. After official ceremonies and special trains the new era officially started on 1 January 1973 when the **Dart Valley Railway Co.** took over using the title 'Torbay Steam Railway' to distinguish it from the other line. The *Flying Scotsman* was brought in as a holiday attraction. More recently, in April 1983, there was an equally glamorous visitor when *Orient Express* Pullman coaches were seen on a 'special' from Paddington at Kingswear for the first time. Now known as the **Torbay and Dartmouth Railway**, it is a summer season only service though there is, at the time of writing, a special diesel service on some Saturdays in March and during the pre-Christmas period.

The last decade has seen only relatively minor physical changes to BR's South Devon system; in 1974 there was storm damage at Dawlish after which the down platform had to be rebuilt. In April 1980 *Tiny*, the last surviving broad-gauge locomotive moved from Newton Abbot to Buckfastleigh. In May that year the 'open station' experiment started; in this the friendly ticket-collectors at station entrances went – and have never returned. Arriving at a strange destination late at night has not been the same since. In 1981 all parcels traffic was abandoned except the Red Star service.[3] 1987 has seen the end of signal boxes on the South Devon lines; the new equipment in Exeter came into use and all the old ones thus became redundant. One gantry, complete with signals, has now been erected as a 'memorial' by railway publisher David St John Thomas at Newton Abbot.

Perhaps the final ignominy of all was the arrival at Paignton in 1985 of the replica of the magnificent *Iron Duke* – the superb broad gauge engine and tender had to be brought in on a standard gauge low-loader and stood on a siding behind the station. Seen in a rainstorm it was the saddest sight of all.

Perhaps a sign of the improving fortunes of British Rail, 1987 has also seen the re-introduction of two named trains from the recent past; linking the North and Midlands to the south west both the *Cornishman* and the *Devonian* are running again after a ten-year break. The *Torbay Express* is also in the timetable again. All are Inter-City 125s.

141

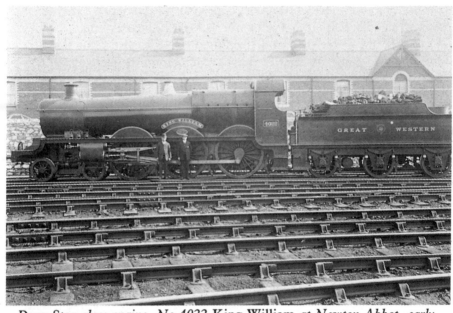

Dean Star *class engine, No 4022* King William *at Newton Abbot, early 1910s (The name-plate is now on display at Pecorama, Beer, Devon)*

Notes to the text

Chapter I   1   Dymond -.*Memoirs*,v.3.Ms in Devon Record Office
2   DRO Plan Ref.104a
3   George,A.G.*James Green, civil engineer, 1781-1849* [in] *Devon Historian No 32,pp.7-14*
4   *Copy with Totnes Community Archive papers*
5   *Booker,F.History of the Great Western Railway*,chap.2
6   Rolt,L.T.C.*Brunel*,p.213
7   Thomas,D.St J.*Regional history of railways*,v.1,pp.25-39
8   Gregory,R.H.*South Devon Railway*,pp.5-7
9   Rhodes,A.J.*Newton Abbot*,p.202
10   DRO Plan Ref.165
11   Copy in Torquay Library
12   Kingdon,A.R.*The Ashburton Branch*,p.53
13   *Torquay Directory*, 28 Feb. 1849
14   Dymond,R. & White,J.T.*A Chronological Record*,p.31
15   Originals in Torquay Library

Chapter II   1   Open to the public during the summer months
2   *See* Bibliography
3   Gregory,R.H,op.cit.,p.19
4   Besley,H.Publisher,*A route book of Devon*
5   Rolt,L.T.C.,op.cit.,p.224
6   Thomas,D.St J.,op. cit.,p.76
7   Hadfield,C.*Atmospheric railways*,p.171
8   MacDermot,E.*History of the GWR*,v.2,p.232
9   *Illustrated London News*, Feb.1855
10   MacDermot,E.,op.cit.,v.2,p.235
11   Gregory,R.,op.cit.,p.42
12   William,K. & Reynolds,D.*The Kingsbridge Branch*,p.5

Chapter III   1   Booker,F.,op.cit.,p.66
2   Winget,W.*Reminiscences of an octogenarian.(Cuttings book in Torquay Museum)*
3   *Ellis,A.C.Historical survey of Torquay*,p.428
4   White,J.T.*History of Torquay,*,p228
5   MacDermot,E,op.cit.
6   *Torquay Directory*,21 Feb. 1849
7   Thomas,D.St J.,op.cit., pp.63-64
8   *Torquay Directory*,30 Dec. 1851

Chapter IV 1 In the Seale papers; copy in Torquay Library
2 *Illustrated London News*, 6 Feb. 1858
3 In Seale papers
4 D&TR letter book in Devon Record Office
5 White,J.T.,op.cit.,pp.231-3
6 White,J.T.,ibid.,p.230
7 White,J.T.,ibid.,p.237
8 Russell,P.*Dartmouth*,p.156
9 Russell,P.,ibid.,p.154
10 Williams, K.& Reynolds,D.op.cit.,pp.27-8

Chapter V 1 Gregory,R.,op.cit.,pp.58-9
2 *Torquay Directory*,May 1870
3 *Torquay Directory*,20 Aug. 1875
4 Rhodes,A.J.,op.cit.,p.204
5 Gregory,R.,op.cit.,p.49
6 *Torquay Directory*,20 Jun. 1883
7 Gregory,R.,op. cit.,pp.65-7
8 Jones, R.*A Book of Newton Abbot*,p.72

Chapter VI 1 Potts,C.R.*The Brixham Branch*,p.15
2 Potts,C.R.,ibid.,pp.15-17
3 Map in possession of the Dart Valley Association
4 Potts,C.R.,op.cit.,pp.21-2
5 MacDermot,E.,op.cit.,v.2.p.241
6 Ewans,A.H.*Haytor Granite Tramway*
7 Ward Lock & Co.*Dartmoor*. 1919-20ed.p.54
8 Thomas,D.St J.,op.cit.,v.1.p.88
9 Kingdon,A.R.*The Ashburton Branch*,p.55
10 Pomroy,L.W.*The Teign Valley Line*.1984
11 DRO Plan Ref.DP 564(Series 1)
12 MacDermot,E.,op.cit.,v.2.p.244

Chapter VII 1 Steel,A.*Jorrick's England*,p.93
2 Simmons,J.*South Western v. Great Western* [in] *Journal of Transport History*,v.5. *pp.13-36*
3 *Dymond,R.& White,J.T.,op.cit.,p.66*
4 *Booker,F.,op.cit.,pp.94-5*
5 *Dymond,R.& White,J.T.op.cit., .p74*
6 *Torquay Directory*,11 Apr. 1883
7 *Torquay Directory*,3 Aug. 1848
8 Booker,F.,op.cit.,pp.103-4

Chapter VIII   1   Ed.by C.Cowan, and privately pub. in Duluth, Mn. 1984
            2   *Great Western Progress, 1835-1935*,p.141
            3   Stanes,R.*History of Devon*,p.114
            4   Booker,F.,op.cit.,p.114
            5   Pack,S.W.C.*Britannia at Dartmouth*,p.168
            6   *Railway Magazine*, Aug. 1908
            7   Pomroy,L.W.,op. cit.,p.71
            8   DRO Plan Ref.DP 674(Series 1)

Chapter IX   1   *Brunel and after*,p.122
            2   *The Great Western Railway: 150 glorious years*,p.153
            3   Ibid.,p.86
            4   Booker,F,.op.cit.,p.149
            5   *Torquay Times*,17 July 1933
            6   Thomas,D.St J.& Smith,S.R.*Summer Saturdays in the West*.1973
            7   *150 glorious years*.Chap.9
            8   *Torquay Times*,25 Jun. 1937
            9   In Torquay Library archives
          10   Balfour,G.*The armoured train*,p.137
          11   Pomroy,L.W.,op.cit.,p.39
          12   Pike,J.R.*Tall Ships in Torbay*,p.127
          13   Pomroy,L.W.,op.cit.,pp.83-4
          14   Booker,F.,op.cit.,p.155

Chapter X   1   Trump,H.*Westcountry harbour*,p.80
            2   *Herald Express*,20 Dec. 1969
            3   Thomas,D.St J.,op.cit.,v.1.p.250

Appendix I   1   DRO Ref.1508M/Devon/Maps/Transport/1
            2   Hadfield,C.*Atmospheric railways*,p.148
            3   A.R. Holman Collection; presented in 1933 [in] Westcountry Studies Library
            4   *Railway Chronicle*,11 April 1848

BIBLIOGRAPHY AND ACKNOWLEDGEMENTS.

There is a considerable bibliography including many books on engines, rolling stock, mainly relating to the Great Western Railway. There are also many smaller but equally valuable books whch are principally pictorial. These can be seen in libraries and bookshops. The list below are histories in the more literal sense and either contain considerable amounts of material on South Devon or deal solely with it.

Allen,G.F.*The Torquay Branch* [in] *Trains Illustrated,* Jul 1958
Ball,E.F.*Some curious railway stations: Dartmouth* [in] *Railway Mag.* vll. 1901. p239
Booker,F.*The Great Western Railway; a new history.* 1977.
Brodribb,J.*Dart Valley's second string.* [in] *Railway Mag.* Dec 1972. p620-4
Camwell,A.A.*Teign Valley Railway* [in] *Railway World,* Feb 1958
Clammer,R.& Kittridge,A.*Passenger steamers of the River Dart.* 1987.
Clayton,H.*The atmospheric railways.* [priv. pr.] 1966
Collins,J.B.B.*Some branch railways in S Devon.* [in] *Railway Mag.* v32. 1913. p131
GWR.*Great Western Progress, 1835-1935.* [1935]
Gregory,R.H.*The South Devon Railway.* 1982.
Hadfield,C.*Atmospheric railways.* 1967. Chaps. 9 & 10
Hall,Jean.*Railway landmarks in Devon.* 1982.
Herald Express.*Transport Bygones.* 1985.
Kingdon,A.R.*The Ashburton Branch (& the Totnes Quay line).* 1977.
MacDermot,E.T.*History of the Great Western Railway.* Rev. by C R Clinker. 3v. 1964
Pomroy,L.*Teign Valley Line.* 1984.
Potts,C.R.*The Brixham Branch.* Oakwood P. 1986.
Railway Correspondence & Travel Soc.*Locomotives of the GWR.* 12 pts.
Roche,T.W.E.*Go Great Western.* Branch Line handbooks. 1966.
Rolt,L.T.C.*Brunel.* 1957.
Sekon,G.A.*History of the GWR.* 1895.
Semmens,P.*History of the GWR, 1923-1948.* 3v. 1985.
Thomas,D.St J.*Regional history of railways.* v1. The West Country. rev. ed.
Thomas,D.St J.& Smith,S.R.*Summer Saturdays in the West.* 1973.
Whitehouse,P.& Thomas,D.St J.*Great Western Railway: 150 glorious years.* 1984.
William,K.& Reynolds,D.*The Kingsbridge Branch.* 1975.
Williams,A.*Brunel and after.* GWR. 1925.

Town histories often contain sections on the local railway; among those consulted have been: Arthur C Ellis's *Historical survey of Torquay.* and his unpublished *History of Brixham*; Roger Jones's *Book of Newton Abbot* and Percy Russell's *Dartmouth*: others are noted in the chapter references.

It is however the newspapers of South Devon which have provided most of the more detailed quotations; where there are parentheses in the text these have been taken from one of the following:

Dartmouth Chronicle from 1855
Herald Express from 1922
Torquay Directory from 1847
Torquay Times from 1869
Trewman's Exeter Flying Post from the 1830s
Western Morning News from 1860

However the most important references are given in the chapter notes.

The company documents of the Dartmouth and Torbay and the Torbay and Brixham Railways appear to have been lost but *Sir* John Seale permitted Devon Library Services to make copies of those in his possession; these are in Torquay Library. Under a House of Commons Order of 1792, confirmed by a 1837 Act, all plans for all *intended* public works were required to be deposited with the Clerk of the Peace. Thus DEVON RECORD OFFICE has virtually a complete record of all railway works (and of schemes which never reached fruition) from 1818 onwards. These are listed in its *Brief Guide*; Part 1 issued some years ago. Some material concerning the South Devon and Teign Valley Railways is in DRO and is listed in the Office's leaflet *Transport History*.

Technical information on engine and rolling stock is in the National Railway Museum, Leeman Road, York. The assistance of the Librarian, Mr C.P.Atkins, is acknowledged with thanks. The definitive collection of books on Devon is in the Westcountry Studies Library (adjacent to Devon Record Office) in Exeter. Among the guides produced by the Librarian is a *Chronological List of Statutes*; this includes almost all the relevant Acts concerning Devon railways. Other lists kept there, including the vast *Burnet Morris Index and the card-index to the Exeter Flying Post*, have been consulted. My special thanks to Mr Ian Maxted for his help and to Mr Michael Dickinson of the Record Office, who provided sources for me not generally known to researchers. A more recent resource is the index created at the Totnes Community Archive, which has been under the able charge of Mr R.Bedward; this government-funded project has now terminated but the more important files are now deposited in Totnes Museum. Finally I would acknowledge the help of my former colleagues, Mr Michael Dowdell and Miss Lorna Smith, at Torquay Area Library, who although always under pressure of work, found time to answer my queries. I owe special thanks too to Tim Dunce who helped greatly with the final editing.

The publisher gratefully acknowledges the help of Donald Jepson, life-long railway buff, for his help in reading the author's text whilst in manuscript form, and for making several useful suggestions.

APPENDIX I.

Atmospheric pumping stations on the South Devon Railway.

A sketch-map in the Courtenay papers[1] depicts eight pumping stations between Exeter and Newton: there were a further three built but were never in operation. Building started under the supervision of Mr P.G.Margery in April 1845 and continued for three years[2] They were:

Exeter.
(Engine supplier: Boulton & Watt) At the south end of St Davids Station; now demolished, it was at one time used for gas-making and had a large water-tank in place of its pitched roof.

Countess Weir.
(Engines: Rennie) 3 miles from Exeter; near the road to 'Trood's lime-kilns'. Demolished many years ago.

Turf.
(Boulton & Watt). 2½ miles from Countess Weir house; near the entrance to the canal [not far from the *Swans' Nest*]. Excavated when a ruin in 1913 after an attempt had been made 'to make out the outline but the walling is covered with earth and overgrown with grass'. *Engine House Pond* was still NW of the site.[3]

Starcross.
(Boulton & Watt) 3 miles from Turf; still in existence and already referred to. During construction there were construction problems, 'the chimney of the engine house has been pulled down and the ground piled so the foundation is now considered secure enough for any thing'.[4]

Dawlish.
(Maudslay's engines) 3½ miles from Starcross: adjacent to the up platform - demolished in the 1850s; there are several good paintings and photographs.

Teignmouth.
(Rennie's) 3 miles from Dawlish. Station built on the east side of Brimley Brook and a new road cut from the station yard to Regent Street. Contemporary prints show the campanile chimney of the engine house rivalling the tower of East Teignmouth Church. Demolished sometime after a sale there in 1858. Lot 1 was 'the Whole of the Materials of the Chimney and Tower (which is beautifully built in Italian Style of Architecture)'. The Engine and Boiler Houses were covered in other lots.

Summer-house.
(Maudsley's) 3 miles from Teignmouth Station near Bishopsteignton. Named because it was near Commyn's Summer House then on the bank of the Teign Estuary opposite Coombe Cellars. Demolished sometime after the 1858 sale; this one included 'TWO large AIR PUMPS', as well as the chimney tower and the two houses.

Newton.
(Rennie's) Just about 2 miles from its neighbour; on the west side of the line there. The building was not demolished until about 1900, although its engine was sold back to its maker in 1853.

The others built but never used were:

Dainton.
Near the west exit of Dainton tunnel: completed in May 1848; engines installed but probably never worked.

Totnes.
Adjacent to the up platform; the boilers were installed but not the rest of the equipment - now part of the Unigate Creamery.

Torquay.
At Longpark beside the Newton-Torquay road; while the building was completed no machinery was installed - probably the best-preserved today. For many years a pottery it is now a fruit wholesaler's warehouse. The subject of an Eden Phillpott's novel entitled *Brunel's Tower.*

APPENDIX II

Some Locomotives used in South Devon, 19th and 20th centuries

Great Western engines
The first ones used by the South Devon were owned by the GWR and were hurriedly brought in when the atmospheric proved a failure.

Name	Class	Built	Details
Pegasus	Fire Fly	1842	2-2-2. 7' driving wheels
Antelope	Sun	1841	2-2-2 6' "
Lance	"	1841	"
Pisces	Leo	1842	2-4-0 5' coupled wheels 1st goods engines
Cancer	"	1841	"
Taurus	"	1841	"
Capricornus	"	1842	
Dromedary	"	1841	"
Scorpio	"	1842	"
Aries	"	1841	"
Stromboli	"	1842	"
Goliath	Hercules	1842	0-6-0 3' coupled wheels 1st 6-coupled engines

Most were withdrawn by 1852, at which time SDR's own were becoming available

South Devon
There were 12 in first contract including:

Comet	1851	Gooch's *Corsair* design
Lance	1851	4-4-0 saddle tanks for
Meteor	1851	passenger use - 5'9"
Aurora	1852	coupled wheels

Later contracts included:

Etna	1855	Similar to Aurora 4-4-0
Hecla	1855	but driving wheels 5'6"
Hawk	1860	Similar to Aurora but
Gazelle	1860	with bigger saddle-tanks
Hector	1860	
Gorgon	1866	Known as Zebra class 4-4-0
Pluto	1866	5'9" driving wheels

Leopard	1872	Same general design but
Stag	1872	suitable for conversion to
Lance	1875	standard-gauge
Osiris	1875	

Lance and *Osiris* replaced earlier engines with the same names

SDR locomotives were not numbered; they were painted dark green with a black panel line and thin white ones on either side. Buffers and buffer beams were vermilion. This is not full list - in all 85 were transferred to the GWR in 1876

Torbay and Brixham

Queen	1852	0-4-0 Bought 1868
Raven	1874	0-4-0 Bought from GWR
	1877	

Great Western Railway

As the hundreds of surviving photographs show, many classes of locomotives have been used on West Country trains; it is therefore possible to list only a selection

Class	*Built*	*Details*
Achilles	1892-9	Dean 2-2-2 (later 4-2-2)
.	.	7'8" driving wheels
Duke	1895-9	Churchward 4-2-2
(sometimes called 'Devons')		
Badminton	1897-9	4-4-0
Bulldog	1899-1910	4-4-0
(Many had 'local' names, e.g. *Dartmouth*, *Torquay* (withdrawn 1934)		
Cities	1903	2-cyl. 4-4-0
e.g *City of Truro*		
Counties	1904	"
Star class, comprising		
Stars	1907	Churchward 4-6-0
Knights	1908	"
e.g. *Knight of St Patrick* seen on the *Torquay Diner* test-run 1908		
Kings & Queens	1909-11	"
Princes & Princesses	1913-4	"
Abbeys	1922-3	"
Saint class, comprising		
Saints	1903-13	Churchward 2-cyl. 4-6-0
Granges	1936-9	"
Manors	1938-50	"

e.g. *Lydham Manor* now in use on the T&DR

Counties	1945-7	″
Halls-50	″	
Castle class	1923-27;1932-39;1946-50 4-6-0	

e.g.*Caerphilly Castle* now in Science Museum. Some became *Earls* after the 32xx 4-4-0s were scrapped. After the Battle of Britain some were renamed after aircraft, e.g. *Spitfire, Hurricane*

King class	1927-30	Collett 4-cyl. 4-6-0

30 of these magnificent passenger engines were built. They had a tractive effort over 40,000lbs. The most famous was *King George V* No 6000, which made the visit to the USA in 1927 and afterwards carried the bell presented by the *Baltimore and Ohio Railroad Company*

There were many unnamed classes, known only by numbers but familiar to many people. These included: 23xx (260 built, in service for 80 years); 41xx (2-6-2T); 43xx (2-6-0 - 342 built) and 45xx (2-cyl. 2-6-2T - 175 built)

British Railways

After nationalisation there was a relatively brief period when steam locomotives of various sizes were again built: as well as those listed above, British standard locomotives were introduced. These included *Britannias* (4-6-2 - allocated to Western Region in 1952, but only occasionally seen in Devon).

Diesel Locomotives

The best known were the diesel-hydraulic locomotives prefaced 'Western' (Class 52). These were withdrawn in the late 1970s and replaced by Class 50s obtained from London Midland Region. The other well-known group was the 'Warships' (some Swindon-built; later Classes 42/3), also diesel-hydraulic and based on a German design. These were phased out in the early 1970s. There was also a similar, but smaller locomotive, known as the Class 22. These were allocated to Laira and Newton Abbot and were frequently seen on the South Devon lines.

Locomotives with pleasant exterior lines were the Beyer Peacock Type 3s (later Class 35); popularly known as 'Hymeks' - these were seen mainly at weekends on holiday trains. Unnamed locomotives included Classes 31 and 47, among others. Although many of the services are now operated by Inter-City (originally HST) 125 units, diesel locomotives are still seen in South Devon; one (unidentified) was seen hauling 13 carriages recently on a mid-week service.

Company/Name	Plans dep	Act	Line opened	Line closed
Torquay, Newton & Ashburton	1832#			
Newton-Torquay	1832	★		
Duke of Somerset's Totnes, Ashburton & Buckfastleigh Rail-Road	1833#			
Bristol & Exeter	1835	1836	1844 (Exeter)	Still operating
Exeter, Plymouth & Devonport	1835#			
North & South Devon	1836#			
London, Exeter & Falmouth	1836	★		
Plymouth, Devonport & Exeter	1840	★		
Devon & Cornwall Central	1841	★		
South Devon(originally the Plymouth, Devonport & Exeter)	1843	1844	1849 (Plymouth)	Still operating
Newton-Torquay	1844	★		
Direct Western Railway	1845	★		
Ashburton, Newton & South Devon Junction	1845	1847		
Later Acts extended line to Torquay and Brixham				
Direct Exeter Plymouth & Devonport	1845#			
Dartmouth, Brixham, Torbay, Exeter & North Devon Junction	1845	★		
South Devon	1846 Amendments & Branches	1846	1848 (Torquay/Tor)	Still operating

Cornwall & Devon Central (and Plymouth)	Pros.1845	1846	*	
Torquay, Brixham & Dartmouth	1852#			
Plymouth, Tavistock, Okehampton				
N Devon & Exeter	1852	*		
Torquay Railway	1852	*		
Dartmouth, Torquay & S Devon	1853	*		(Dartmouth Railway on prospectus)
Torquay & S Devon Railway Ext	1854	*		
Dartmouth & Torbay	1856	1857	1864 (Dartmouth)	Closed from Paignton 1972 now T&DR. To P'ton still BR
Kingsbridge & S Devon	1858	*		
Torquay Railway [Horse tramway]	1859# submitted	Bill		
Plymouth & South Hams	1859	*		
Devon Central	1860	*		
Kingsbridge (& Salcombe)	1863	1864 (Repealed 1886)		
Teign Valley	1862-78	Various	1882 (Heathfield-Ashton) 1903 (Exeter)	1958
Torbay & Brixham	1863	1864	1868	1963
Buckfastleigh (Totnes) & S Devon	1863/4	1864/6,1868	1872	1958
Totnes-Ashburton				Opened 1969 as DVR Totnes-Buckfast'h
Totnes-Totnes Quay				Goods only; worked by horses until 1874.

Totnes, Ashburton,
Buckfastleigh & Newton 1863 ★
South Hams 1864#
S Devon (Exeter City
   Basin) 1864   1864   1867   See Chap. 6
Moretonhampstead & Sq
   Devon 1864   1862,1872   1867   1958
                                                      Track retained
                                                     to Heathfield.

Exeter, (Teign Valley)
& Chagford 1877/82/94   1883
Plymouth, Totnes,
Paignton & Torquay 1879-93   1880
                          1897   Act abandoned
                                    1884
Kingsbridge & Salcombe 1881   1882,1887/   powers vested in
                                GWR; constr. under New   Lines Act,
                                1888   1893   1963
Brent,Ashburton &
   Heathfield 1897   ★
(Mid Devon Railway)

Exeter Railway 1902   1903   1958
                                      as cont. of
                                      Teign Valley
Devon, South Hams
   Light R 1899   ★

Key

No plans deposited; preliminary moves only made
★ No progress made after plans deposited
Every effort has been made to make this a complete list. Other companies may have been formed which had a very limited life, and therefore have escaped notice, as the Journals of the House of Lords and House of Commons have not been searched.

INDEX